신경림 – 농 무

Farmers' Dance

Poems by Shin Kyŏng-Nim

Translated by Brother Anthony of Taizé /Young-Moo Kim

도서 출판 답게

Farmers' Dance

Translated by Brother Anthony of Taizé / Young-Moo Kim

This bilingual edition is a joint publication of DapGae Publishing Company and the Cornell University East Asia Program. Number 105 in the Cornell East Asia Series (ISSN 1050-2955), Cornell University East Asia Program, 140 Uris Hall, Ithaca, NY 14853-7601.

Tel 607-255-6222 / Fax 607-255-1388

Published by DapGae Books
201 Won Bld
829-22 Bangbae 4-dong, Socho-ku, Seoul 137-064 Korea
Tel / (02)591-8267, 532-4867, 537-0464, 596-0464 Fax / 594-0464

Cornell East Asia Program
Cornell University
Ithaca, New York 14853

No.105, Cornell East Asia Series ISSN 1050-2955
Cornell East Asia Program ISBN 1-885445-05-9

DapGae

English Translations
of Korean Literature Series

Editor : Young-Moo Kim

차　례

Contents

머리말　*INTRODUCTION*

1

2

3

4

5

6

7

『한국문학 영역총서』를 펴내며

머리말

신경림은 1935년 한국의 충청북도 충주에서 태어났다. 한국의 옛 농촌문화 가운데서 자라난 신경림은 성장한 후 지방의 여러 곳을 여행하면서 시골 마을에 전해 내려오는 노래들을 모았다. 그가 시인으로 등단한 것은 1956년《문학예술》에 "갈대"를 포함한 세 편의 시가 출판되면서이다. 그러나 첫 작품들이 발표된 후 여러 해 동안 그는 단 한 편의 시도 발표하지 않은 채, 민중 노동자의 세계로 들어가 농부, 광부, 상인 등으로 일하였다. 이 기간 동안 얻은 경험들은 그의 가장 뛰어난 작품들의 밑바탕에 깔려 있다. 신경림은 서른이 넘은 1967년에야 동국대학교 영문학과를 졸업했다.

신경림의 시인으로서의 명성은 1973년 출간된 시집『농무』에 주로 기인하고 있다. 이 시집에 수록된 시 중 몇 편은 1970년에 전위적인 계간지《창작과 비평》에 처음 발표되어 그의 문학계로의 귀환을 장식한 작품들이다. 한국 현대시의 발달에 있어 이 시집이 가지는 역사적 의의는 실로 엄청나다고 할 것이다. 1974년, 『농무』는 신경림에게 제1회 "만해문학상"을 안겨주면서 그의 작품에 기대하지 않았던 명성과 비평적 관심이 집중되는 계기가 되었다. 이로써 신경림은 가혹한 사회 현실에 뿌리를 둔 시가 대중에게 받아들여지는 데에 공헌했으며, 이러한 전투적인 문학은 이후 80년대 노동시로 발전하였다.

『농무』에 수록된 작품 중 다수는 불특정한 복수의 화자에 의해 이

야기된다. "우리"로 나타나는 이 화자는 종종 "민중"이라 지칭되는, 시인 자신이 생활을 함께 했던 빈곤층, 농민, 노동자, 광부 등을 아우르는 집단적 주체이다. 그가 자신을 이들의 대변인으로 내세우는 것은 단순한 공감에 기초한 것이 아니다. 그는 진정 그들의 일원으로서 그들의 가난과 고통, 소박한 기쁨과 좌절된 희망들을 나누었다. 신경림은 현대 한국의 첫 민중시인들 중 한 명이다. 그가 환기시키는 쓰라림이 신경림 자신이 내면으로부터 직접 겪었던 것이라는 의식은 그의 시들이 지닌 힘을 한층 더해준다.

『농무』에는 1945년 광복 이후 한국사를 특징짓는 정치적 폭력의 기억이 시집 전체를 통해 되풀이되고 있다. 해방 첫 해의 분열과 갈등은 결국 육이오 전쟁(1950~3)으로 절정에 이르렀고, 전쟁 후 60년대와 70년대를 통한 정부의 산업화 정책은 전란으로 인해 이미 심각한 혼란을 겪은 농촌의 인구를 다시 한 번 잔인하게 뿌리뽑으면서, 폭력이 지속되는 결과를 낳았다. 그리고 이 때에는 점점 더 가혹해져 가던 박정희 대통령의 독재 아래 모든 형태의 정치적 저항과 조직 결성이 금지되고 맹렬히 억압되었다. 특히, 노동자의 권리에 대한 그 어떠한 주장도 공산주의로 치부되고 북한의 지원을 받는 것으로 간주되어 국가보안법에 의해 범죄로 처벌받았다.

서구 낭만주의 전통의 개인주의적 1인칭 화자나 한국 현대 서정시의 정체가 모호한 화자에 익숙해져 있는 문학 풍토 속에서, 『농무』의 집단적 "우리"는 매우 충격적으로 받아들여졌다. 60, 70년대의 저명한 한국 시인들은 프랑스 상징주의에서 영감을 받은 고도로 심미적인 문체의 시를 쓰고 있었다. 시인과 비평가들은 입을 모아 문학이 정치적,

사회적 쟁점들과 직접적인 관련을 맺어서는 안 된다고 주장했다. 이 주장은 1960년대 초 젊은 작가와 비평가들에 의해 이미 비판받은 바 있었다. 그 젊은 문학인들 중에는 신경림에게 영향을 주었으며 1968년 자동차 사고로 작고한 시인 겸 비평가 김수영도 포함되었는데, 특히 일상의 언어의 구어적 간결성을 보존하는 시를 옹호한 김수영의 주장은 신경림의 작품들에 투영되어 있다.

『농무』는 진부한 문학적 관습에 대한 김수영의 거부를 새로운 차원으로 끌어올렸으며, 맹렬한 비평적 논의를 불러일으켰다. 이제 문학계가 크게 나뉘면서, 좀더 행동주의적이고 '참여적인' 작가들은 사회참여를 주장하는 그들만의 문학 운동을 확립하였다. 신경림은 이 운동에서 지도적 역할을 계속해왔으며 민족문학작가회의와 한국민족예술인총연합의 의장을 역임하였다. 이들 단체의 회원들은 70년대와 80년대를 통해 여러 차례 체포되고 또 고초를 겪었다.

『농무』의 시 중 많은 작품들은 한국 빈곤층의 아픔과 상처를 강렬한 감수성으로 표현해낸다. 시집 앞부분의 작품들은 주로 벽지의 가난한 이들에 관한 것이고, 뒷부분의 작품들에서는 산업사회에서 변두리로 내몰린 도시 빈곤층에 초점이 맞추어져 있다. 1973년 발행된 『농무』의 초판에는 농촌 생활의 모습을 담은 40편 남짓한 작품이 실렸다. 2판(1975)에서는 1973~75년 사이에 좀더 도시적인 맥락에서 제작된 20여 편의 작품이 2부로 나뉘어 추가되었다. 일부 비평가들은 후에 쓰인 작품들이 힘이 떨어진다고 지적하며 이러한 확장을 부정적으로 보기도 하지만, 제2판 증보판이 시인의 최종적 선택을 보여준다는 의미에서 여기서는 후자를 완역 수록하였다.

농무 이후에 출판된 신경림의 시집으로는 『새재』 (1979)와 『달넘세』 (1985), 『가난한 사랑노래』 (1988), 『길』 (1990), 『어머니와 할머니의 실루엣』 (1998) 등이 있다. 신경림은 다가가기 쉬운 율동적인 언어로, 때로는 무당의 주문에 가까운, 때로는 서울에서는 아니라 해도 시골 마을에서는 아직까지 불려지고 있는 민요들을 연상케하는 가락이 있는 이야기시를 지어낸다. 그의 작품 중 상당 부분은 19세기 말과, 일제 시대, 또는 지난 50년 간의 혼란기 동안 시인의 고향인 남한강 기슭의 농민들이 겪어온 고통을 서사시적 틀로 엮어내고 있다.

이제까지 어떤 시인도 신경림만큼 시골과 도시를 막론한 민중의 특징적인 목소리를 훌륭하고 겸허하게 표현해낸 이는 없었다. 그는 결코 자신의 시에 등장하는 이들을 감상적으로 그리는 법이 없다. 오히려 그는 독자로 하여금 물리적, 문화적 외양을 넘어 그들을 지극히 예민하고 또한 고통받는 인간으로서 바라볼 수 있도록 한다.

이 시들은 시 자체로서 그리 이해하기 어려운 작품들이 아니다. 대부분은 주의 깊은 독자에게 자명한 내용의 시들이다. 그러나 동시에 이 시들은 한국 농촌의 문화적 특수성에 깊숙이 뿌리박고 있으며, 또한 이 시들은 어느 정도는 아직도 살아 있는 그와 같은 과거의 삶에 익숙한 독자들을 상정한다. 한국인이 아닌 사람들에게는 이러한 삶을 경험할 기회가 많지 않기 때문에, 그러한 독자들을 위해 몇 가지를 미리 설명하는 것이 도움이 될 듯하다. 이 책에서는 각각의 시에 해설을 달기보다는 독자가 필요로 할 만한 정보들을 이 서론에 모아놓았다.

번역을 하면서 우리는 다른 문화나 영어에는 대응될 만한 말이 없는 단어들을 여럿 다루어야 했다. 이와 같은 단어들 중 일부는 한글 그대로 남겨두었으며, 여기에 그 의미에 대한 간단한 해설을 덧붙이기로 하였다. 이 낱말들은 단순히 독립된 번역상의 문제가 아닌, 그들이 사용되는 문화 자체의 표현들이다. 한국 문화는 그 어느 곳의 문화와도 정확히 일치하지 않으며, 중국이나 일본의 문화와 혼동되어서는 안될 것이다.

번역이 불가능한 단어들 중 일부는 징, 꽹과리, 벅구, 날라리 등 악기의 이름이다. 한국 농촌 사회에서 음악은, 다른 모든 삶의 국면들과 마찬가지로, 종교적인 차원을 지닌다. 여기서 근본이 되는 종교 정신은 샤머니즘이라고 부를 수 있는, 이로운 귀신들과 해로운 귀신들이 있다는 믿음이다. 매년 되풀이되는 파종과 수확의 기간 중간중간에는 시끄러운 타악기 음악이 터져나온다. 이는 논밭에서 혹은 마을의 마당과 거리들에서 연주되며, 이로운 귀신들을 북돋고 해로운 귀신들을 쫓기 위한 것이다. 이 음악의 박자는 듣는 이에게 춤을 추고 싶은 뿌리칠 수 없는 충동을 불러일으키며, 흥에 취한 일종의 몽환상태로 이끌기도 한다. 한국 농민들의 춤은 주로 손과 팔을 들어 이를 엎었다 뒤집었다 하는 동작으로 이루어지는데, 여기서 어깨의 들썩임은 결정적인 역할을 한다. 발의 움직임은 별로 없고, 춤추는 이들은 제 자리에서 몸을 돌리고, 서로 건드리지 않는다.

춤을 이끄는 농악대가 쓰는 악기는 그 수가 많지 않다. 그 중 몇몇은 금속으로 되어 있다. 기본 박자는 징이 잡아주는데, 이는 지름이 18인치 이상 되는 굵은 소리와 울림을 가진 타악기로서, 한 악절이 시작될 때마다 치게 된다. 그 위로 음악의 주된 흐름은 2개 이상의 꽹과리가 만들어나간다. 꽹과리는 손에 들고 단단한 막대기로 쳐 칭칭 소리를 내는 작은 징인데, 매우 다양한 패턴의 리듬으로 때로는 리듬을 주고받으면서, 또 때로는 서로 겨루면서 연주된다.

농악에 사용되는 다른 악기로는 여러 종류의 북이 있는데, 그 중 가장 작은 벅구를 제외하고는 작품에서 직접 언급되지는 않는다. 그 외에 날라리라 불리는 악기도 있다. 날라리는 혀(reed)가 두 개가 달렸다는 점에서는 오보에나 클라리넷과 비슷하나 그 소리는 훨씬 강렬하고 날카로워, 춤의 절정에서 긴 음을 연속적으로 뽑아냄으로써 소란스런 타악기들의 소리를 뚫고 들리도록 만들어졌다. 연주하는 사람과 춤추는 사람, 그리고 관객간에는 뚜렷한 구분이 없다. 춤은 단체적인 성격을 띤다. 일반적으로 연주자들은 남성이지만, 대부분의 젊은 여성들이 둘러서서 구경하는 동안, 좀더 나이가 많은 여자들은 함께 춤에 끼기도 한다.

농촌 지방, 특히 서남부 쪽은 풍부한 민요의 보고이다. 그 가운데서 '육자배기'만이 작품 속에 직접적으로 언급되어 있다. 가난한 이들의 아픔과 인내를 힘찬 음색으로 표현하고 있는 이 노래는 곳곳에 여러 가지 형태로 존재한다. 많은 전통 민요들은 가난하고 불우한 이들의 고통을 노래하고 있는데, 신경림은 특히 이러한 노래들에 꾸준한 관심을 가져왔으며, 우리는 주제뿐만 아니라 그 리듬의 반향을 신경림의 시 속에서 들을 수 있다.

시 번역과 이해에 있어 문제가 될 수 있는 또 다른 부분은 먹을 것과 마실 것이다. 한국인의 주식은 밥이며, 배추나 기타 야채를 소금에 살짝 절인 후 고춧가루, 생강, 새우젓 등의 재료로 간을 맞추어 일정

기간 발효시켜서 만드는 '김치'와 함께 상에 오른다.

가난해서 쌀을 살 돈이 없거나 너무 지쳐서 요리를 할 수 없을 때는 언제나 '라면'이라는 해결책이 있다. 봉지에 넣어 싼 값에 판매되는 이 음식은 마을 구멍가게라면 어디에서든 살 수 있으며, 공장에서 건조 처리된 면과 양념을 위한 분말 수프를 함께 물에 넣고 몇 분 간 끓이기만 하면 완성된다. 라면은 매우 인기있는 식품이지만 영양가는 거의 없다.

시 속에 언급되는 또 하나의 면 음식으로 국수가 있다. 이는 좀더 두껍고 부드러운 면으로서, 종종 약간의 고기와 야채가 첨가된 국물에 담겨 잔치음식이나 스낵으로 애용된다. 면은 밀가루나 다른 분쇄된 곡류로 만들어진다.

술은 이 시들뿐만 아니라 한국인의 삶에서 큰 역할을 한다. 술은 항상 단체로 마시며, 혼자 마시는 법은 거의 없다. 예전에 가장 즐겨 마시던 술은 '막걸리'였다. 이 술은 쌀로 빚는데, 하루 일을 끝낸 후 즐기기 위해서뿐만 아니라 일손을 잠시 멈출 때 기운을 돋우기 위해서도 애용되었다. 작품 속에 나오는 주된 술은 막걸리보다 상당히 세고 작은 잔에 담아 마시는 값싼 무색의 증류주 '소주'이다. 소주는 아직도 저녁 때면 남자들이 모여 으레 마시곤 하는 술이다. 맥주는 한국 농촌문화의 일부가 아니었으며, 여기에 실린 시 중에 맥주에 대한 언급이 없는 것 또한 주목할 만한 점이다.

한국 사람들은 술을 마실 때면 꼭 돼지고기나 마른 오징어, 문어 등의 음식을 곁들인다. 이러한 맥락에서 몇 차례 언급되는 또 다른 요리로 '묵'이 있다. 묵은 도토리를 갈아 물에 끓여 응고시킨 일종의 갈색 젤리이며, 차게 식힌 후 얇게 썰어서 간장으로 양념해먹는다. 도토리는 야생으로 자라고 마음대로 딸 수 있으므로 묵은 가난한 이들의 음식으로 인식되어 있다. 저장해놓은 곡식이 바닥이 나가고 신선한 채소가 없는 늦겨울에 묵이 있다는 것은 크게 다행한 일이었다.

술을 마시는 장소는 다양하다. 마을 가게에서 술을 사면 바로 문 밖에 준비된 자리에서 마시든지 아니면 다른 곳으로 가져가서 마실 수 있다. 길가 주점에도 술을 마실 수 있는 최소한의 공간이 마련되어 있는데, 겨우 앉을 만한 자리와 술잔을 놓을 데가 있을 뿐이다. 그 다음으로는 실내에 방이 있는 좀더 큰 규모의 술집들이 있다. 그리고 마지막으로 값비싼 술집들이 있다. 이런 종류의 술집에서는 젊은 여자들이 술을 대접하며, 노래와 춤, 그리고 기타의 방법을 통해 손님들을 즐겁게 해주도록 되어 있기 때문에 한두 군데에서는 '창부집'이라는 이름으로 언급되기도 한다.

한국의 달력은 서양에서는 '중국설날'로 알려져 있는 음력 새해와 함께 시작된다. 음력 1월 1일은 보통 양력 2월에 걸린다. 이 날 사람들은 조상들께 제물을 올리고 자기 나이에 한 살을 더한다 (이는 아기들이 태어나는 순간 인생의 첫 해를 맞이하므로 처음부터 '한 살'이라는 관점에서이다). 음력 8월 보름은 수확의 달이라 하여 '추석'이라는 명절을 쇤다. 추석이 되면 가족을 돌보아주심에 대한 감사의 표시로 조상들께 제물을 올린다. 조상의 기일에도 역시 제물이 올려진다. 제사는 집안의 여자들이 밤새도록 준비한 한 상의 음식을 아침에 올리고 그 앞에서 남자들이 (보통 여자는 제외된다) 순서대로 절을 하고 곡주를 바치는 것으로 이루어진다. 그 다음엔 참석한 모든 사람들이 제사 음식을 나눠 먹게 된다. 집안 남자들은 종종 술을 마시고 화투를 치며, 한국 남성들의 사교적 어투를 특징짓는 크고 걸걸한 목소리로 대화를 나누며 밤을 지새곤 한다.

한국의 풍경에는 곳곳에 죽은 이의 무덤(영문으로는 종종 "tomb"이라고 번역된)이 눈에 띄는데, 이들은 주로 남쪽을 면한 언덕바지에 위치한다. 전통적으로 공동묘지는 없으나, 한 가족의 일원들은 특별히 사놓은 선산에 같이 장사 지내는 일이 많다. 관을 묻은 자리를 덮는 봉분은 평민을 위한 작은 크기의 것으로부터 왕족을 위한 거대한 능에 이르기까지 다양하다. 아이들과 천민의 묘는 아무런 표지를 하지 않았다. 성묘는 집에서 치르는 제사의 연장으로서, 음식을 차리고 절을 한 다음 곡주를 올리게 된다.

전통적으로 사용된 달력은 음력이지만, 이 외에도 태양력에 따른 계절의 변화를 지칭하는 24개의 절기가 있으며 이들은 음력의 변화를 따르지 않는다. 신경림의 시에 언급된 절기로는 2월 말경 동면하던 개구리가 땅 위로 나옴으로써 겨울의 끝을 알린다는 경칩(驚蟄), 그리고 8월 말경 한여름 무더위의 끝을 알리는 처서(處暑)가 있다.

작품 속에 그려지는 풍경은 유럽이나 미국의 그 어떤 풍경과도 다르다. 한국의 경치에는 드넓게 펼쳐진 평야가 거의 없다. 국토의 대부분이 줄에 줄을 잇는 가파른 돌산으로 덮여 있으며, 적어도 이들의 낮은 지대까지는 나무들이 자라고 있다. 비가 오면 급류로 변하는 시내들로 인해 깎인 계곡이 많다. 험한 지형으로 인해 교통이 어려웠으므로, 20세기 전 한국에는 잘 닦여진 큰 길이 전혀 없었다. 한국의 언덕은 워낙 가파르기 때문에, 높이가 1,000미터를 넘는 경우가 거의 없음에도 불구하고 영어로 이들을 '산(mountains)'이라고 부르는 것이 일반화되었다.

마을은 보통 지형이 경작에 실용적일 만큼 평탄해지는 곳에 서 있다. 가끔씩 깊은 골짜기 외딴 거주지들이 있기도 하다. 작품에서는 종종 장이 서는 비교적 큰 규모의 마을들이 등장한다. 7일로 이루어진 일주일의 단위는 흔히 사용되지 않았으며, 아직까지도 장은 종종 5일 주기로 서곤 한다. 장이 서는 자리는 평소엔 비어 있으며, 보따리 장사꾼들과 상인들은 다른 날 장이 서는 인근 마을로 옮겨 다닌다. 장의 주위에는 작은 방들이 들어찬 좁은 골목들이 있어서 사람들은 이곳에서 먹고 마시게 된다.

한국 전통 가옥의 몇몇 특징이 또한 시에서 언급되고 있다. 이러한 집들은 빠른 속도로 사라져가고 있다. 1970년대까지 대부분의 집들은 짚단을 두껍게 덮어 지붕을 올렸다. 벽은 엮은 윗가지와 흙을 발라 만들거나 볏단을 썰어 진흙과 섞어 좀더 단단하게 만들었다. 집의 내부를 잇는 복도는 없었다. 방들은 모두 마당으로 바로 통해 있었으며, 처마로 가려질 만큼의 좁다란 툇마루가 방문 앞으로 빙 둘려졌다. 이 툇마루는 어른이 앉아서 다리를 드리울 수 있을 정도로 꽤 높았는데, 이 아래의 땅에는 신발을 놓았다.

방들은 방바닥 아래로부터 난방을 하는 온돌 장치로 인해 지면보다 높게 올려졌다. 집의 한 쪽 끝에 위치한 부엌에서 시작한 열과 연기는

돌로 된 바닥을 통과해 반대편 끝의 굴뚝으로 배출되었다. 비교적 큰 집들에는 흔히 '대청마루'가 있었다. 대청마루는 지붕으로 덮인 나무 바닥으로서, 사람들은 여름이면 이곳에 앉을 수 있었다. 각각의 방에는 흰 종이를 바른 격자무늬 문창살을 한 미닫이문이 달려 있었다. 창문도 비슷한 방식으로 종이를 발라 만들어졌는데, 창문 유리라는 것은 알려진 바가 없었다.

시 속에 나타난 기후는 극과 극을 달린다. 여름의 기온은 섭씨 35도를 넘기도 하는 반면, 겨울에는 모진 추위가 닥쳐 때로는 기온이 영하 30도에 달하기도 한다. 겨울이 오면 어느 정도의 눈이 오며, 산 속에는 더 많은 눈이 내린다. 늦은 6월과 이른 7월은 장마철로서, 큰비가 자주 내린다. 그 결과, 여름은 더울 뿐만 아니라 극도로 습해서 상당히 불쾌감을 준다. 9월부터 11월 중순이나 하순까지 계속되는 긴 가을은 밝은 햇빛과 깊고 푸른 하늘이 있는, 한국의 가장 아름다운 계절이다.

이 시집의 작품들에서 소박한 사람들의 삶이 주요 배경을 이루는 반면, 한국사의 주요 사건들은 거의 언급되지 않는다. 그러나 직접 드러나지만 않을 뿐 커다란 역할을 하고 있다. 몇몇 중요한 날짜들이 있다. 1910년부터 1945년 사이 한국은 일본의 지배하에서, 특별히 잔인한 방식으로 합병, 식민지화되었다. 이는 1919년 3월 1일 한국 전역에 걸친 만세운동을 촉발했으며, 이 운동은 사나운 탄압에도 불구하고 계속되었다. 매년 3월 1일은 이 운동을 기념하는 날이다.

연합군은 제2차세계대전 중 한국에 상륙하지는 않았으나, 일본에게 항복과 동시에 한국에서 철수할 것을 요구했다. 따라서 일본이 항복한 날인 1945년 8월 15일은 국가가 광복을 맞은 날로 기념된다. 연합국은 한국이 완전한 민족국가로 자리잡도록 이끄는 책임을 소련과 미국이 나눌 것에 합의하고는 북쪽에 소련을, 남쪽에 미국을 진주시켰다. 남쪽 측은, 김일성의 주도하에 공산 정권이 권력을 잡아가던 북측의 참여 없이, 이승만의 지도로 1948년 대한민국을 설립했다.

1950년 6월 25일, 북측 정권의 군대는 남쪽을 침공하였다. 이렇게 시작된 한국전쟁(육이오 전쟁)은 평화협정이 체결되지 않았으니까, 현재까지 계속되고 있는 셈이다. 1953년 휴전협정이 38도선과 그 주변을 따라 나라의 분계선을 확정짓게 되었을 땐 이미 300만여 명이 죽음을 당한 후였다.

이승만은 헌법에서 규정한 임기가 끝나는 1960년까지 대통령직을 수행했다. 이승만 정권은 부패로 악명이 높았으므로, 그가 새로운 임기를 시작할 의사를 보이자 서울과 전국 각지에서는 고등학생과 대학생을 포함한 분노한 국민들이 집단 시위를 벌였다. 1960년 4월 19일, 군대가 비무장 학생들에게 발포하여 수많은 인명을 살상하였다. 이승만은 하야할 수밖에 없었고, 민주주의의 새로운 새벽이 곧 다가올 듯이 보였다.

그러나 1961년 5월 16일, 박정희가 이끄는 군대는 쿠데타를 일으켜 정권을 장악했다. 박정희는 1979년 10월 29일 암살당할 때까지 독재자 대통령으로 군림했다. 그의 정권은 일제에 의해 시작되었던 도시화, 산업화 과정에 박차를 가했다. 1960년에 한국은 광물자원을 거의 가지고 있지 못한, 세계에서 가장 가난한 나라 중 하나였다. 경제학자들은 '한국의 기적'을 말하곤 하지만, 여기에 수록된 시들은 동일한 사건들을 판이한 관점에서 보여준다.

도시화는 농촌 마을들의 인구 고갈을 불러왔다. 빈곤이 일반화되어 있던 당시, 기본 식량의 가격은 자연히 낮았다. 농부들은 가난했으며, 그 중 다수가 자신의 땅을 갖지 못하고 다른 사람 소유의 경지를 일구어 생계를 이어나갔다. 사람들은 불법으로 산 속에 약간의 땅을 개간하여 야채를 심기도 했다. 산업화가 시작되자 임금은 최저 수준으로 유지되어야 했고, 이는 도시에서 식량의 가격이 그에 상응하도록 낮게 유지되어야만 사회안정이 지속될 수 있음을 의미했다. 또 이는 결과적으로 농부들의 소득이 전혀 없음을 의미했다.

젊은이들은 마을을 떠나 새로운 산업지대에서 저임금 건축인부나 기술이 없는 막일꾼으로 일자리를 구할 수밖에 없었다. 서울의 신흥 부유층은 가정부를 필요로 했고, 시골 처녀들은 이러한 기대에 이끌려 서울로 모여들었다. 하지만 이들은 결국 술집과, 용산 이외에도 많았던 홍등가 지구에 종착하기 일쑤였다.

가난으로 인한 고통이 이 시집에 실린 시들의 주된 사회적 주제 중 하나이다. 거기엔, 도망칠 곳이 없다는, 어딜 가도 인생이 더 나아지지 않을 것이라는 느낌이 깃들어 있다. 동시에, 이 시들은 그 안에 그려진 소박한 사람들의 강렬한 인간성을 엿보게 해준다. 이들의 인간적인 모습은 소박한 친근함, 기쁜 일과 슬픈 일, 그리고 주먹다툼에서까지도, 서로 인정을 나누는 삶을 영위하는 모습을 통해 드러난다.

멸시당하는 한국의 가난한 이들에게서 서정시에 적합한 소재를 찾아냈다는 것은, 부분적으로 사회주의적 사고의 영향이 없지 않으나, 혁명

적인 일보였다. 이 시들의 영향력은 그만큼 컸으며, 이름 없는 한국의
민중을 노래했다는 점에서 온 세계의 독자들에게 읽힐 만한 가치를 지
닌다.

안 선 재 (안토니 수사)

Introduction

Brother Anthony

Shin Kyŏng-Nim was born in 1935 in Ch'ungju, North Ch'ungch'ŏng Province, in South Korea. He grew up in the midst of Korea's old rural culture and in later years went travelling about the countryside, collecting the traditional songs of the rural villages. His literary career as a poet officially dates from the publication in 1956 in the review *Munhak Yesul* of three poems, including "The Reed" but for years after that he published nothing, immersing himself instead in the world of the working classes and working as a farmer, a miner, and a merchant. The experience of those years underlies much of his finest work as a poet. He only graduated from the English Department of Dongkuk University (Seoul) in 1967, when he was over thirty.

His fame as a poet dates mainly from the publication of the collection *Nong-mu* (Farmers' Dance) in 1973, some of the poems from which were first published in the avant-garde review *Ch'angjak-kwa Pip'yŏng* in 1970, heralding his return to the literary scene. It would be difficult to exaggerate the historical significance of this volume in the development of modern Korean poetry. In 1974 *Nongmu* earned Shin the first Manhae Literary Award, bringing his work unexpected publicity and critical attention. Shin thus helped open the way for public acceptance of a poetry rooted in harsh social realities, a militant literature that was to grow into the workers' poetry of the 1980s.

Many of the poems in this collection are spoken by an undefined plural voice, a "we" encompassing the collective identity of what is sometimes called the *Minjung*, the poor people, farmers, laborers, miners, among whom the poet had lived. He makes himself their spokesman on the basis of no mere sympathy; he has truly been one of them, sharing their poverty and pains, their simple joys and often disappointed hopes. Shin is one of the first non-intellectual poets in modern Korea and the awareness that he knows the bitterness he is evoking from the inside gives his poems added power.

Echoing throughout *Nong-mu* are memories of the political violence that has characterized Korea's history since its Liberation from Japanese rule in 1945. The divisions and conflicts of the first years of independence culminated in the Korean War (1950~3). Later, throughout the 1960s and 70s, the government's policy of industrialization led to a further brutal uprooting of rural populations that had already undergone severe dislocation in the course of the war, and violence continued. In those years, all forms of political opposition or social organization were forbidden and fiercely suppressed under the increasingly severe dictatorship of President Park Chung-Hee. In particular, any advocacy of workers' rights was considered to be an expression of communism, a sign of support for North Korea, and was punished as a crime against national security.

In a literary culture accustomed to the individualistic "I" speaker of the western romantic tradition, or the fairly unspecified voice of modern Korean lyrics, the collective "we" employed in *Nong-mu* was felt to be deeply shocking. The leading recognized Korean poets in the 1960s and 1970s were writing in a highly esthetic style inspired by certain aspects of French Symbolism. Poets and critics alike insisted that literature should have no direct concern with political or social issues. This had already been challenged in the earlier 1960s by a number of younger writers and critics including the poet and essayist Kim Su-Yŏng, who was killed in a car crash in 1968. In particular, Kim's advocacy of a poetic style reflecting ordinary, everyday spoken language, with its colloquialisms and pithiness, is reflected in Shin's poems.

Nong-mu took Kim's rejection of conventionally accepted literary style to new heights and gave rise to an intense critical debate. A major literary scission occurred and the more activist, 'engaged' writers established their own movement, advocating social involvement. Shin Kyŏng-Nim has continued to play a leading role in this movement. He has served as president of the Association of Writers for National Literature, and of the Federation of Korean Nationalist Artists. Members of these groups were repeatedly arrested and harrassed throughout the 1970s and 80s.

The poems of *Nong-mu* often express with intense sensitivity the pain and hurt of Korea's poor, those of remote villages in the earlier sections, but the final poems focus in part on the urban poor, those marginalized in industrial society. The first edition of *Nongmu* published in 1973 contained just over forty poems, mainly written years earlier and full of echoes of rural life. A second edition (1975) added two extra sections containing nearly twenty poems written between 1973 and 1975, in a more urban context. Some critics regret this expansion, feeling that these poems are less powerful, but the fuller version represents the poet's final option and is here translated in its entirety

Later volumes of Shin's poetry include *Saejae* (1979), *Talnomse* (1985), *Kananhan sarangnorae* (1988), *Kil* (1990) and *Halmŏni wa ŏmŏni ŭi silhouette* (1998). Shin uses easily accessible, rhythmic language to compose lyrical narratives that are at times close to shamanistic incantation, or at others recall the popular songs still sung in rural villages if not in Seoul. Much of his work composes a loosely framed epic tale of Korean suffering, as experienced by the farmers living along the shores of the South Han River, the poet's home region, in the late 19th century, during the Japanese colonial period, and during the turmoil of the last fifty years.

No poet has so well expressed, and so humbly, the characteristic voice of Korea's masses, both rural and urban. Shin never sentimentalizes his subjects but rather takes the reader beyond the physical and cultural exterior to reveal them as intensely sensitive, suffering human beings.

These poems, as poems, are not very difficult to understand, they can mostly speak for themselves to the attentive reader. Yet at the same time, they are deeply rooted in the cultural particularities of the Korean countryside. They assume a readership familiar with the life that was and, to some extent at least, still is lived there. Few non-Koreans have had a chance to see and experience that life, and for them a few explanations may prove helpful. Rather than provide notes to individual poems, we have brought together the information that a reader may need in this introduction.

The translators have had to deal with a series of words that have no equivalent in other cultures or in the English language. We have chosen to keep certain words in Korean and to offer here a brief indication of their meaning. The words are not mere isolated translation problems, they are expressions of the culture in which they are used. Korean culture has no exact parallels elsewhere, it should not be confused with the cultures of China or Japan.

Some of the untranslateable words are names of musical instruments: *ching, kkwengkwari, pokku, nallari.* In Korea's rural communities, music, like every aspect of life, has a religious dimension. The fundamental religious spirit may be termed Shamanistic, the belief that there are spirits which help and spirits which cause harm. The annual rythm of seed-time and harvest is punctuated by bursts of noisy percussion music played by the men out in the fields or in the streets and yards of the village, designed to encourage the good spirits and discourage the harmful ones. The rhythms of this music easily provoke an irresistible desire to dance, and this can put people into a kind of trance. The Korean farmers' dance is done mainly with the hands and arms twisting in the air, with the rocking of the shoulders playing a vital role. The feet move little, the dancer turns while remaining on the spot. Dancers do not touch one another.

The team of musicians leading the dance usually have a small set of instruments. Some are made of metal: the basic rhythm is set by the *ching*, a deep-voiced, resonant gong 18 inches or more in diameter that is beaten at the start of each musical phrase; over this, the main musical flow is the work of two or more *kkwenggwari,* small rattly gongs held in the hand and beaten with hard sticks in a great variety of rhythmical patterns, at times engaging in dialogue or competition with one another.

Other instruments used include various kinds of drum, not named in these poems, with the exception of the *pokku,* the smallest kind. In addition, there is the *nallari,* a kind of oboe or clarinet in that it uses a double reed, but far more strident, designed to pierce through the clamor of percussion instruments in a series of sustained notes at the climax of the dance. There is no clear distinction between musicians, dancers, and spectators, the dance is communal and although the players are usually men, the older women will also join in, while younger women mostly stand watching.

The rural areas, especially in the south-west, are rich in popular songs of which only one, the *yukjabegi* is mentioned explicitly. This exists in many versions, it expresses the pain and endurance of the poor in vibrant tones. Shin Kyŏng-Nim has always been particularly interested in such songs and their rhythms echo in his poetry, as well as their themes, for many traditional songs are evocations of the sufferings of the poor and unfortunate.

Another major source of potential difficulty involves food and drink. The Korean staple diet is rice, which is eaten with *kimch'i*, a preparation of uncooked long-leafed cabbage or other vegetables salted lightly, then seasoned by the addition of powdered red pepper husks, ginger, shrimp paste, and other ingredients, then allowed to ferment for a time.

When someone is too poor to buy rice, or is too tired to cook, there is always *ramyŏn*, cheap packs of industrially produced dried noodles sold in every village store, that need only to be boiled in water for a couple of minutes, with the contents of a little packet of powdered stock added to give taste. *Ramyŏn* is very popular but has little nutritive value.

Another kind of noodle mentioned in the poems is *kuksu*, a thicker kind of soft noodle, often served at parties or as a snack, where the soup in which the noodles are served may include a little meat and fresh vegetables. Noodles are made from wheat or other kinds of flour.

Drinking plays a big role in these poems, and in Korean life; it is always communal, almost never solitary. The most popular drink used to be *makkŏlli*, made of rice and drunk in pauses during work to give energy, as well as after work for pleasure. The main drink mentioned in the poems is *soju*, a cheap colorless distillate considerably stronger than *makkŏlli*, drunk from small glasses. It is still the main drink of men drinking of an evening. Beer was not part of rural Korean culture. Its absence from these poems is significant.

Koreans never drink alcohol without eating something: pork, dried squid or octopus. Another dish mentioned in this connection several times is *muk*, a brown jelly made by boiling up flour made from acorns and served cold, sliced, seasoned with soy sauce. The acorns grow wild, and can be gathered freely, so that *muk* is recognised as a food of the poor. It was especially valued toward the end of winter, when stores of grain were running low and no fresh plants were available.

Drinking is done in various places. In the village store, bottles can be bought to be drunk on a space arranged just outside, or to be taken away. Roadside bars also offer a minimal space for drinking, just something to sit on and a place for the glasses. Then come the larger establishments with rooms indoors. Finally there are the more expensive houses, where the drink is served by young girls who are also expected to entertain the customers by singing and dancing, and in other ways too, so that the term "whore-houses" has once or twice been introduced.

The Korean year begins with the Lunar New Year, known in the West as the Chinese New Year. This usually falls in February. It is the day when offerings are made to ancestors, and everyone adds one year to their age, since babies are born into their first year and so are "one year old" at birth. The full moon of the eighth month is celebrated as the Harvest Moon, *Ch'usŏk*, when offerings are made to the ancestors in thanks for their care for the family. Offerings are also made on the anniversary of deaths. They involve the all-night preparation by the women of a table of food, which is then offered in the early morning when the men (not usually the women) make a series of prostrations and take turns in presenting cups of rice-wine. The food is then eaten by all those present. The menfolk have often spent the whole night drinking, playing cards, and talking in the loud, hearty voices that characterize Korean male social discourse.

The graves of the dead (often termed "tombs" in English translation) are scattered across the Korean landscape, mostly on south-facing hillsides. Traditionally there were no communal graveyards, although members of a family are often buried together on a hill bought for that purpose. The circular earthen tumulus above a burial varies in size from a small mound for the humble to a large hillock for royalty. The graves of children and people of the lowest classes were left unmarked. Visits to the grave prolong the celebration of offerings at home; food is laid out, prostrations are made, and wine is offered.

Although the traditional calendar was lunar, there is also a set of twenty-four days with names indicating the stages of the solar climate, that does not follow the variations of the lunar calendar. Such dates mentioned in Shin Kyŏng-Nim's poems include *Kyŏng-chip* when frogs are thought to mark the end of winter by emerging from hibernation late in February, and *Ch'ŏsŏ* which heralds the end of the extreme summer heat late in August.

The landscape evoked in the poems is very unlike that found in Europe or America. The Korean landscape has very few open plains. Most of the territory is covered with range upon range of steep rocky hills, wooded at least in the lower reaches. There are many valleys carved out by streams that become rushing torrents after rain. The roughness of the terrain makes travel difficult, there were no highways in pre-20th century Korea. Because of their steepness, it has become customary to call the Korean hills "mountains" in English, although few are more than a thousand meters high.

The villages usually stand at points where the land levels out enough for paddy-fields to be practicable, although there are also isolated settlements in the hills. The poems often evoke the larger towns where markets are held. The seven-day week was not a familiar measure of time, and markets still often take place on a five-day rhythm. The market areas remain empty on the other days, the peddlers and merchants moving on to nearby towns where markets are held on other dates. Around the market are little alleys lined with small rooms where people eat and drink.

The traditional Korean house has certain characteristic features that are mentioned in the poems. These houses are rapidly disappearing. Until the 1970s most houses were roofed with a thick layer of rice-straw. The walls were made with wattle and daub, or a more solid mixture of clay and straw. There were no inside corridors, each room gave directly on to the yard, with a fairly narrow wooden step or platform sheltered by the eaves running around the house in front of the doors. Shoes were left on the ground below the step, which was quite a high one, high enough for an adult to sit with legs hanging down.

The rooms were raised above ground level by the *ondol* system of underfloor heating. The heat and smoke from the fire in the kitchen at one end of the house passed under the stone floors, heating them before emerging through a chimney at the other end. In larger houses there would also often be a *maru*, an open space with a wooden floor, covered by the roof, where people could sit in the summer. Each room was closed by a sliding door of open fretwork to which white paper was pasted. The windows were similarly covered with paper; window glass was unknown.

The climate evoked in the poems is extreme. The summer temperatures can rise beyond 35 degrees, while the winters are bitter, sometimes reaching minus 30 degrees Celsius. Winter brings a certain amount of snow, more in the mountains. In late June and early July there is a rainy season when heavy downpours are common. As a result the summer is not only hot but extremely humid and therefore unpleasant. The long autumn, lasting from September until mid or late November, is Korea's most beautiful season, with bright sunlight and deep blue skies.

Compared to the humble human setting, the main events of Korean history are not mentioned in the poems, but they play a major unspoken role. Certain dates are important. From 1910 until 1945, Korea was under Japanese rule, annexed and colonized in a particularly ruthless manner. This provoked an Independence Movement which was launched across Korea on March 1, 1919 and continued despite fierce repression. March 1 is the day when this movement is commemorated.

The Allied Forces never landed in Korea during World War II but demanded that Japan should withdraw from it on surrendering. The date of the Japanese surrender, August 15, 1945 is therefore hailed as the day of National Liberation. The allies agreed that the USSR and the USA should share responsibility for the land's transition to full nationhood, the USSR in the north, the USA in the south. In the south a Republic was set up in 1948 under the leadership of Syngman Rhee but without the participation of the northern areas, where a Communist regime was taking power, led by Kim Il-Sung.

On June 25, 1950, the armed forces of the regime installed in the northern part invaded the south, opening the Korean War which still continues, no peace treaty having been signed. Before the 1953 Armistice froze the division on the country along or near the 38th Parallel, some three million people had died.

Syngman Rhee continued as president of the Republic of Korea until 1960, when he was due to reach the end of his constitutional mandate. His regime had become notoriously corrupt, so when he indicated his intention of taking a new term in power, popular indignation was expressed by popular demonstrations including high school and college students, in Seoul and elsewhere. The armed forces opened fire on the unarmed students on April 19, 1960, killing many. Syngman Rhee was obliged to step down and it seemed that a new dawn of democracy was at hand.

On May 16, 1961, the military led by Park Chung-Hee staged a coup and he took power, continuing as president-dictator until his assassination on October 26, 1979. During his rule, the process of urbanization and industrialization begun under the Japanese was intensified. Korea was one of the poorest countries of the world in 1960, with few mineral resources available in the south. Economists talk of a "Korean Miracle" but these poems show the same events from a very different perspective.

Urbanization led to the depopulation of the villages. Since poverty was general, the price of basic foodstuffs was naturally low. Farmers were poor; many had no land of their own but depended on work in the fields belonging to others. People would illegally clear a small patch of land in the hills in which to plant some vegetables of their own. When industrialization began, wages had to be kept at minimum levels and this meant that social peace could only be preserved if the price of food in the cities were kept equally low. This in turn meant that the farmers in the villages could still earn almost nothing.

Young people were thus encouraged to leave the villages to look for work in the new industrial sector, as poorly paid construction workers or unskilled laborers. The new wealthy class in Seoul wanted housemaids, and village girls were lured to Seoul by this prospect. Very often they ended up in bars and on the streets of the red-light areas of which Yongsan was only one.

The sufferings caused by poverty are one of the main social themes of these poems, with the feeling that there is no escape, nowhere to go where life might be better. At the same time the poems suggest that the simple people evoked in them are intensely human, a humanity expressed by their ability to share life together in simple friendliness, in joys, in sorrows, and even in fist-fights.

It was a revolutionary step, only partly inspired by socialist currents of thought, to find in the lives of Korea's despised poor a worthy subject for lyric poetry. The influence of these poems has been correspondingly immense and in their celebration of Korea's nameless masses they deserve a worldwide audience.

1

겨울밤

우리는 협동조합 방앗간 뒷방에 모여
묵내기 화투를 치고
내일은 장날. 장꾼들은 왁자지껄
주막집 뜰에서 눈을 턴다.
들과 산은 온통 새하얗구나. 눈은
펑펑 쏟아지는데
쌀값 비료값 얘기가 나오고
선생이 된 면장 딸 얘기가 나오고.
서울로 식모살이 간 분이는
아기를 뱄다더라. 어떡헐거나.
술에라도 취해 볼거나. 술집 색시
싸구려 분 냄새라도 맡아 볼거나.
우리의 슬픔을 아는 것은 우리뿐.
올해에는 닭이라도 쳐 볼거나.
겨울밤은 길어 묵을 먹고.
술을 마시고 물세 시비를 하고
색시 젓갈 장단에 유행가를 부르고
이발소집 신랑을 다루러
보리밭을 질러 가면 세상은 온통
하얗구나. 눈이여 쌓여
지붕을 덮어 다오 우리를 파묻어 다오.
오종대 뒤에 치마를 둘러 쓰고
숨은 저 계집애들한테

On a Winter's Night

We're met in the backroom of the co-op mill
playing cards for a dish of *muk*;
tomorrow's market-day. Boisterous merchants
shake off the snow in the inn's front yard.
Fields and hills shine newly white, the falling snow
comes swirling thickly down.
People are talking about the price of rice and fertilizers,
and about the local magistrate's daughter, a teacher.
Hey, it seems Puni, up in Seoul working as a maid,
is going to have a baby. Well, what shall we do?
Shall we get drunk? The bar-girl smells
of cheap powder, but still, shall we have a sniff?
We're the only ones who know our sorrows.
Shall we try raising fowls this year?
Winter nights are long, we eat *muk,*
down drinks, argue over the water rates,
sing to the bar-girl's chop-stick beat,
and as we cross the barley-field to give a hard time
to the newly-wed man at the barber's shop, look:
the world's all white. Come on snow, drift high,
high as the roof, bury us deep.
Shall we send a love-letter
to those girls behind the siren tower hiding

연애 편지라도 띄워 볼거나. 우리의
괴로움을 아는 것은 우리뿐.
올해에는 돼지라도 먹여 볼거나.

wrapped in their skirts? We're

the only ones who know our troubles.

Shall we try fattening pigs this year?

시골 큰집

이제 나는 시골 큰집이 싫어졌다.
장에 간 큰아버지는 좀체로 돌아오지 않고
감도 다 떨어진 감나무에는
어둡도록 가마귀가 날아와 운다.
대학을 나온 사촌형은 이 세상이 모두
싫어졌다 한다. 친구들에게서 온
편지를 뒤적이다 훌쩍 뛰쳐 나가면
나는 안다 형은 또 마작으로
밤을 새우려는 게다. 닭장에는
지난 봄에 팔아 없앤 닭 그 털만이 널려
을씨년스러운데 큰엄마는
또 큰형이 그리워지는 걸까. 그의
공부방이던 건넌방을 치우다가
벽에 박힌 그의 좌우명을 보고 운다.
우리는 가난하나 외롭지 않고, 우리는
무력하나 약하지 않다는 그
좌우명의 뜻을 나는 모른다. 지금 혹
그는 어느 딴 나라에서 살고 있을까.
조합 빚이 되어 없어진 돼지 울 앞에는
국화꽃이 피어 상그럽다 그것은
큰형이 심은 꽃. 새 아줌마는
그것을 뽑아내고 그 자리에 화사한
코스모스라도 심고 싶다지만

Country Relatives

Nowadays I hate our uncle's place down in the country.
Once uncle's at market he's slow coming home,
rooks flock fit to darken the sky, cawing
in the persimmon tree that's dropped all its fruit.
My cousin, a college graduate, says he hates
the whole world. When he suddenly goes rushing out
after browsing through letters from friends, I know
he's off to an all-night game of mahjong again.
The chicken coop looks bleak,
with just a few feathers left drifting from the chickens
sold off last spring. I wonder if my aunt
misses her eldest son? Clearing out what used to be
his study-room on the other side of the yard, she cries
at the sight of the mottoes he wrote on the wall:
We may be poor, we're not lonely; We're
powerless but not weak, only I don't understand
what the words mean. I wonder
if he's living in some other country now?
The pigs have gone to pay off co-op debts.
In front of their sty chrysanthemums bloom bright.
My oldest cousin planted them. Now his wife
wants to pull them up and sow pretty
cosmos in their place and I hate

남의 땅이 돼 버린 논뚝을 바라보며
짓무른 눈으로 한숨을 내쉬는 그
인자하던 할머니도 싫고
이제 나는 시골 큰집이 싫어졌다.

my grandmother too: she used to be so kind, now
she keeps gazing at the ridges in the sold-off fields
and sighing away with watery eyes.
Nowadays I hate our uncle's place down in the country.

遠隔地

박서방은 구주에서 왔다 김형은 전라도
어느 바닷가에서 자란 사나이.
시월의 햇살은 아직도 등에 따갑구나.
돌이 날으고 남포가 터지고 크레인이 운다.
포장 친 목로에 들어가
전표를 주고 막걸리를 마시자.
이제 우리에겐 맺힌 분노가 있을
뿐이다. 맹세가 있고 그리고 맨주먹이다.
느티나무 아래 자전거를 세워 놓은
면서기패들에게서 세상 얘기를 듣고.
아아 이곳은 너무 멀구나, 도시의
소음이 그리운 외딴 공사장.
오늘밤엔 주막거리에 나가 섰다를
하자 목이 터지게 유행가라도 부르자.
사이렌이 울면 밥장수 아주머니의
그 살찐 엉덩이를 때리고 우리는
다시 구루마를 밀고 간다.
흙먼지를 뒤집어 쓰고 밀린 간조날을
꼽아 보고. 건조실 앞에서는 개가
짖어 댄다 고추 널린 마당가에서
동네 아이들이 제기를 찬다. 수건으로
볕을 가린 처녀애들은 킬킬대느라
삼태기 속의 돌이 무겁지 않고

Lands Far Apart

Old Park's from Kuju. Kim's a fellow
grew up in some Chŏlla coastal place.
The October sunshine still stings our backs.
Stones fly, dynamite blasts, cranes whine.
Let's go to the bar there under its awning,
hand in our chits, drink some *makkŏlli.*
All we've got left now is our pent-up fury,
nothing more. Just oaths and naked fists.
We hear tales of outside from the council clerks
who dump their bikes beneath the big tree.
Oh, this place is too remote, we miss the city's
din here in this god-forsaken construction site.
Tonight let's get out to the bars down the road,
play cards, belt out songs at the top of our voices.
The siren wails; one final slap at the fat behind of
the woman who cooks in the chop-house,
and off we go, dragging our carts along,
covered in dust, counting the days
till pay day. Outside the drying room a dog
is barking; down the sides of the yard
where red peppers lie drying, the village kids
play at *ch'egi* using their feet. The girls,
keeping the sunlight off their heads with a towel,

십장은 고함을 질러 대고. 이 멀고
외딴 공사장에서는 가을 해도 길다.

giggle away the weight of the stones in their panniers;
the foreman yells at the top of his voice. In this remote
far-off construction site the autumn sun is slow to set.

씨름

난장이 끝났다. 작업복
소매 속이 썰렁한 장바닥.
외지 장꾼들은 짐을 챙겨
정미소 앞에서 트럭을 기다리고
또는 씨름판 뒷전에 몰려
팔짱을 끼고 술렁댄다.

깡마른 본바닥 장정이
타곳 씨름꾼과 오기로 어우러진
상씨름 결승판. 아이들은
깡통을 두드리고 악을 쓰고
안타까워 발을 동동 구르지만
마침내 나가 떨어지는 본바닥
장정. 백중 마지막 날.

해마다 지기만 하는 씨름판
노인들은 땅바닥에 침을 배알다.
타곳 씨름꾼들은 황소를 끌고
장바닥을 돌며 신명이 났는데

학교 마당을 벗어나면
전깃불도 나가고 없는 신작로.
씨름에 져 늘어진 장정을 앞세우고

Wrestling

The bustling market's done. The market-place wind
blows chill up overall sleeves.
The visiting merchants have packed up their goods
and are waiting in front of the mill for the truck,
or crowd the back rows round the wrestling ring
with folded arms and anxious murmurs.

The last bout, the deciding match, pits
the toughness of one scrawny native lad
against a visiting wrestler. The kids
bang tin cans and scream,
stamp in disappointment, but in the end
it's the native lad who gets overthrown.
The last day of *Paekjung*, the late summer festival.

The old men round the ring spit in disgust:
why, they lost every year.
In great glee the visiting team try to lead
the ox they won round the market place

but once outside the school yard
there's only the unlit highway.
Tired of the smell of *ch'amoi* and watermelons,

마을로 돌아가는 행렬은
참외 수박 냄새에도 이제 질리고
면장집 조상꾼들처럼 풀이 죽었다.

the men parade back to the village,
the weary looser leading the way, crestfallen
like mourners at a magistrate's house.

罷場

못난 놈들은 서로 얼굴만 봐도 흥겹다
이발소 앞에 서서 참외를 깎고
목로에 앉아 막걸리를 들이켜면
모두들 한결같이 친구 같은 얼굴들
호남의 가뭄 얘기 조합 빚 얘기
약장사 기타 소리에 발장단을 치다 보면
왜 이렇게 자꾸만 서울이 그리워지나
어디를 들어가 섰다라도 벌일까
주머니를 털어 색싯집에라도 갈까
학교 마당에들 모여 소주에 오징어를 찢다
어느새 긴 여름해도 저물어
고무신 한 켤레 또는 조기 한 마리 들고
달이 환한 마찻길을 절뚝이는 파장

After Market's Done

We plain folk are happy just to see each other.
Peeling *ch'amoi* melons in front of the barber's,
gulping down *makkŏlli* sitting at the bar,
all our faces invariably like those of friends,
talking of drought down south, or of co-op debts,
keeping time with our feet to the herb peddlar's guitar.
Why are we all the time longing for Seoul?
Shall we go somewhere and gamble at cards?
Shall we empty our purses and go to the whore-house?
We gather in the school-yard, down squid with *soju.*
In no time at all the long summer day's done
and off we go along the bright moonlit cart-track
carrying a pair of rubber shoes or a single croaker,
    staggering home after market's done.

제삿날 밤

나는 죽은 당숙의 이름을 모른다.
구죽죽이 겨울비가 내리는 제삿날 밤
할일 없는 집안 젊은이들은
초저녁부터 군불 지핀 건넌방에 모여
갑오를 떼고 장기를 두고.
남폿불을 단 툇마루에서는
녹두를 가는 맷돌 소리.
두루마기 자락에 풀 비린내를 묻힌
먼 마을에서 아저씨들이 오면
우리는 칸데라를 들고 나가
지붕을 뒤져 참새를 잡는다.
이 답답한 가슴에 구죽죽이
겨울비가 내리는 당숙의 제삿날 밤.
울분 속에서 짧은 젊음을 보낸
그 당숙의 이름을 나는 모르고.

The Night We Make Offerings

I don't know what dad's dead cousin's name was.
The night we make the offerings for him,
          winter rain is gloomily pattering down
and the younger relations, having nothing else to do,
gather in a side room where the floor's been heated
to gamble at cards or play chess.
From the lamplit verandah rises the sound
of a hand-mill churning out a slurry of green beans.
When our uncles arrive from their distant home,
their greatcoats full of the stink of grass,
we go out with lanterns and delve
into the roof-thatch after nestling sparrows.
Tonight's dad's cousin's offerings; winter rain
patters down in my heavy heart.
Dad's cousin spent a miserable short life
and I don't even know what his name was.

農舞

징이 울린다 막이 내렸다
오동나무에 전등이 매어달린 가설 무대
구경꾼이 돌아가고 난 텅빈 운동장
우리는 분이 얼룩진 얼굴로
학교 앞 소줏집에 몰려 술을 마신다
답답하고 고달프게 사는 것이 원통하다
꽹과리를 앞장세워 장거리로 나서면
따라붙어 악을 쓰는 건 쪼무래기들뿐
처녀애들은 기름집 담벽에 붙어 서서
철없이 킬킬대는구나
보름달은 밝아 어떤 녀석은
꺽정이처럼 울부짖고 또 어떤 녀석은
서림이처럼 해해대지만 이까짓
산구석에 처박혀 발버둥친들 무엇하랴
비료값도 안나오는 농사 따위야
아예 여편네에게나 맡겨 두고
쇠전을 거쳐 도수장 앞에 와 돌 때
우리는 점점 신명이 난다
한 다리를 들고 날나리를 불거나
고갯짓을 하고 어깨를 흔들거나

Farmers' Dance

The *ching* booms out, the curtain falls.
Above the rough stage, lights dangle from a paulownia tree,
the playground's empty, everyone's gone home.
We rush to the *soju* bar in front of the school
and drink, our faces still daubed with powder.
Life's mortifying when you're oppressed and wretched.
Then off down the market alleys behind the *kkwenggwari*
with only some kids running bellowing behind us
while girls lean pressed against the oil shop wall
giggling childish giggles.
The full moon rises and one of us
begins to wail like the bandit king Kŏkjŏng; another
laughs himself sly like Sŏrim the schemer; after all
what's the use of fretting and struggling, shut up
        in these hills
with farming not paying the fertilizer bills?
Leaving it all in the hands of the women,
we pass by the cattle-fair, then dancing
in front of the slaughterhouse
we start to get into the swing of things.
Shall we dance on one leg, blow the *nallari* hard?
Shall we shake our heads, make our shoulders rock?

꽃 그늘

소주병과 오징어가 놓인
협동조합 구판장 마루
살구꽃 그늘.

옷섶을 들치는
바람은 아직 차고
'건답 직파' 또는

'농지세 1프로 감세'
신문을 뒤적이는
가난한 우리의 웃음도
꽃처럼 밝아졌으면.

소주잔에 떨어지는
살구꽃 잎.
장터로 가는 조합 마차.

Shadows of Flowers

Apricot blossom shadows fall
across the old wooden planks of the co-op porch
where a bottle of *soju* and some dried squid lie.

The breeze lifting our coat-collars
is still pretty chilly and I only wish
that the laughter of us poor folks,

laughing to read "Plant rice in dry fields"
and "One percent off the farmland tax"
as we browse through the newspapers,
would grow as bright as those flowers up there.

One apricot petal
falls into the glass.
The union cart's on its way to market.

눈길

아편을 사러 밤길을 걷는다
진눈깨비 치는 백 리 산길
낮이면 주막 뒷방에 숨어 잠을 자다
지치면 아낙을 불러 육백을 친다
억울하고 어리석게 죽은
빛 바랜 주인의 사진 아래서
음탕한 농지거리로 아낙을 웃기면
바람은 뒷산 나뭇가지에 와 엉겨
굶어 죽은 소년들의 원귀처럼 우는데
이제 남은 것은 힘없는 두 주먹뿐
수제빗국 한 사발로 배를 채울 때
아낙은 신세 타령을 늘어 놓고
우리는 미친놈처럼 자꾸 웃음이 나온다

Snowy Road

I walk through the night, off to buy opium.

Down a long mountain trail in driving sleet,

sleeping by day hidden in the back rooms of inns.

When I'm weary, I call the woman in to play cards.

When I make her laugh with my suggestive jokes

under the faded photo of the landlord

who was falsely accused and stupidly killed,

the wind entangles itself in the branches of trees

on the hill behind and weeps

like the sorrowful ghosts of lads that starved

and now all I have left is two powerless fists.

As I fill my stomach with a bowl of dumpling soup

the woman goes on and on bewailing her lot

and we keep laughing out loud like two mad fools.

어느 8月

빈 교실에서 누군가 오르간을 탔다
빨래바위 봇물에 놓은 어항에는
좀체 불거지들이 들지 않아
배꼽에도 차지 않는 물에 드나들며
뜨거운 오후를 참외만 깎았다
해가 설핏하면 미장원 계집애들이
고기잡는 구경을 나와
마침내 한데 어울려 해롱대었으나
써늘한 초저녁 풀 이슬에도 하얀
보름달에도 우리는 부끄러웠다
샛길로 해서 장터로 들어서면
빈 교실에서는 오르간 소리도 그치고
양조장 옆골목은 두엄 냄새로
온통 세상이 썩는 것처럼 지겨웠다

One August

Someone was playing the harmonium
in the empty classroom.
Minnows wouldn't enter the fish-trap we'd set up
in the stream dammed by a laundry-stone, so
we kept dashing into the water,
that didn't come up to our belly-buttons,
and peeling *ch'amoi* melons in the warm afternoon.
When the sun declined the beauty-parlor girls
came out to watch us fishing
and ended up frolicking about with us
but we felt ashamed of the dew
on the early evening grass
and of the full moon too.
When we took a byway back to the market square
the harmonium had stopped playing
in the empty classroom
and the lane by the brewery stank of manure
as if the whole world was rotting away.

잔칫날

아침부터 당숙은 주정을 한다.
차일 위에 덮이는 스산한 나뭇잎.
아낙네들은 뒤울안에 엉겨 수선을 떨고
새색시는 신랑 자랑에 신명이 났다.
잊었느냐고, 당숙은 주정을 한다.
네 아버지가 죽던 날을 잊었느냐고.
저 얼빠진 소리에 귀 기울여 뭣하랴.
마침내 차일 밑은 잔칫집답게 홍청대어
새색시는 시집 자랑에 신명이 났다.
트럭이 와서 바깥 마당에 멎었는데도
잊었느냐고, 당숙은 주정을 한다.
네 아버지가 죽던 꼴을 잊었느냐고.

Party Day

Dad's cousin's been drunk and rowdy since daybreak.

Cheerless leaves are falling on the awning.

Women clustered in the back yard are making a fuss,

the excited bride's boasting about her new husband.

Have you forgotten? Dad's cousin's drunk and rowdy.

Have you forgotten the day your father died?

No point in listening to his stupid voice.

Finally a proper party comes alive beneath the marquee,

the excited bride's boasting about her in-laws.

Even though the truck's arrived, drawn up in front:

Have you forgotten? Dad's cousin's drunk and rowdy.

Have you forgotten how your father died?

장마

온 집안에 퀴퀴한 돼지 비린내
사무실패들이 이장집 사랑방에서
중돈을 잡아 날궂이를 벌인 덕에
우리들 한산 인부는 헛간에 죽치고
개평 돼지비계를 새우젓에 찍는다
끗발나던 금광시절 요릿집 얘기 끝에
음담 패설로 신바람이 나다가도
벌써 예니레째 비가 쏟아져
담배도 전표도 바닥난 주머니
작업복과 뼛속까지 스미는 곰팡내
술이 얼근히 오르면 가마니짝 위에서
국수내기 나이롱뻥을 치고는
비닐 우산으로 머리를 가리고
텅 빈 공사장엘 올라가 본다
물 구경 나온 아낙네들은 우릴 피해
녹슨 트랙터 뒤에 가 숨고
그 유월에 아들을 잃은 밥집 할머니가
넋을 잃고 앉아 비를 맞는 장마철
서형은 바람기 있는 여편네 걱정을 하고
박서방은 끝내 못 사준 딸년의
살이 비치는 그 양말 타령을 늘어 놓는다.

Summer Rains

The whole house is full of a thick stench of pig.
The clerks have slaughtered a piglet, kill time
in the visitors' room at the village captain's house,
so we carriers from Hansan are free to stay in the store
where we dip our share of pig's lard in shrimp sauce.
After talk of eating out in prosperous gold-mining days
a dirty joke raises a boisterous laugh but
it's been pouring with rain for nearly a week,
our pockets have run out of fags and vouchers
a mouldy stench has soaked into overalls and bones.
Drinking till we're tipsy, we play cards on the mats
to see who will pay for the *kuksu* noodles.
Later, covering our heads with plastic umbrellas,
we climb up to the vacant construction site.
The women out to view the water avoid us,
hiding behind the rusty tractor, while the old woman
at the canteen who lost her son in June
sits there heedless, drenched in the monsoon rains.
Old So is worrying about his flighty wife, and Pak
is spinning tales of stockings he never bought, so fine
his daughter's flesh would have shown right through.

오늘

국수 반 사발에
막걸리로 채워진 뱃속
농자천하지대본
농기를 세워놓고
면장을 앞장 세워
이장집 사랑 마당을 돈다
나라 은혜는 뼈에 스며
징소리 꽹과리 소리
면장은 곱사춤을 추고
지도원은 벅구를 치고
양곡 증산 13.4프로에
칠십 리 밖엔 고속도로
누더기를 걸친 동리 애들은
오징어를 훔치다가
술동이를 엎다
용바위집 영감의 죽음 따위야
스피커에서 나오는
방송극만도 못한 일
아낙네들은 취해
안마당에서 노랫가락을 뽑고
처녀들은 뒤울안에서
새 유행가를 익히느라
목이 쉬어

Today

Stomachs full with half a bowl of *kuksu* noodles
washed down with *makkŏlli,*
banners planted with slogans proclaiming
Agriculture is the Nation's Foundation
we're dancing round the village head's front yard
with the county magistrate leading the way,
our gratitude to the nation deep in our bones
as the magistrate dances the hunchback's dance
to tinkling *kkwenggwari* and booming *ching*
and the instructor bangs away on a *bokku*
for our 13.4% increase in grain production
an expressway less than twenty miles off
and local kids dressed in tattered rags
swipe dried octopus
upend crocks of wine
the drama broadcast through the village speakers
is much better fun than the news
that the old man down at Dragon Rock has died
the womenfolk are drunk
as they sing on and on in the inner yard
while the younger girls out at the back
practice new songs
until they're hoarse

펄럭이는 농기 아래
온 마을이 취해 돌아가는
아아 오늘은 무슨 날인가
무슨 날인가

and ah, I wonder, who knows
what day today is
with the entire village out dancing, drunk
under fluttering banners?

2

갈길

녹슨 삽과 괭이를 들고 모였다
달빛이 환한 가마니 창고 뒷수풀
뉘우치고 그리고 다시 맹세하다가
어깨를 끼어 보고 비로소 갈길을 안다
녹슨 삽과 괭이도 버렸다
읍내로 가는 자갈 깔린 샛길
빈 주먹과 뜨거운 숨결만 가지고 모였다
아우성과 노랫소리만 가지고 모였다

The Way to Go

We gathered, carrying rusty spades and picks.
In the bright moonlit grove
behind the straw sack storehouse,
first we repented and swore anew,
joined shoulder to shoulder; at last we knew
which way to go.
We threw away our rusty spades and picks.
Along the graveled path leading to the town
we gathered with only our empty fists and fiery breath.
We gathered with nothing but shouts and songs

前夜

그들의 함성을 듣는다
울부짖음을 듣는다
피맺힌 손톱으로
벽을 긁는 소리를 듣는다
누가 가난하고
억울한 자의 편인가
그것을 말해 주는 사람은
아무도 없다 달려 가는 그
발자국 소리를 듣는다
쓰러지고 엎어지는 소리를
듣는다 그 죽음을 덮는
무력한 사내들의 한숨
그 위에 쏟아지는 성난
채찍소리를 듣는다
노랫소리를 듣는다.

The Night Before

Hearing their cries.
Hearing screams.
Hearing the sound of bloody nails
clawing at walls.
Who wants to take the side
of the poor and downtrodden?
Nobody wants to talk
of those things. Hearing the sound
of footsteps racing away.
Hearing the sound of people collapsing,
falling. The sound of helpless
men's sighs covering those deaths,
hearing above them the sound
of furious whiplashes raining down.
Hearing the sound of songs.

폭풍

자전거포도 순댓국집도 문을 닫았다
사람들은 모두 장거리로 쏟아져 나와
주먹을 흔들고 발을 굴렀다
젊은이들은 징과 꽹과리를 치고
처녀애들은 그 뒤를 따르며 노래를 했다
솜뭉치에 석웃불이 당겨지고
학교 마당에서는 철 아닌 씨름판이 벌어졌다
그러다 갑자기 겨울이 와서
먹구름이 끼더니 진눈깨비가 쳤다.
젊은이들은 흩어져 문 뒤에 가 숨고
노인과 여자들만 비실대며 잔기침을 했다
그 겨우내 우리는 두려워서 떨었다
자전거포도 순댓국집도 끝내 문을 열지 않았다

The Storm

The bicycle store and the *sundae* soup shop closed.
All the inhabitants came pouring out into the marketplace
shaking their fists and stamping their feet.
The younger ones went pounding on *jing* and *kkwenggwari*
while the lasses came following behind them singing.
Lighting torches made of cotton wadding soaked in oil
they set up an out-of-season wrestling match
　　　　in the school yard.
But then suddenly winter arrived
dark clouds gathered and dropped damp sleet.
The young men scattered and hid indoors,
only the old and the women tottered about, coughing.
All winter long we shook for dread.
And in the end the bicycle store and the *sundae* soup
　　　　shop failed to re-open.

그날

젊은 여자가 혼자서
상여 뒤를 따르며 운다
만장도 요령도 없는 장렬
연기가 깔린 저녁길에
도깨비 같은 그림자들
문과 창이 없는 거리
바람은 나뭇잎을 날리고
사람들은 가로수와
전봇대 뒤에 숨어서 본다
아무도 죽은 이의
이름을 모른다 달도
뜨지 않은 어두운 그날

That Day

One young woman all alone
follows weeping behind a bier.
A procession with no funeral banners,
no hand-bell in front. Ghost-like shadows
along the smoke-veiled evening road,
a breeze scattering falling leaves
down alleys with neither doors nor windows,
while people watch hiding
behind telegraph posts and roadside trees.
Nobody knows the dead
man's name that dark
and moonless day.

山1番地

해가 지기 전에 산 일번지에는
바람이 찾아 온다.
집집마다 지붕으로 덮은 루핑을 날리고
문을 바른 신문지를 찢고
불행한 사람들의 얼굴에
돌모래를 끼어얹는다.
해가 지면 산 일번지에는
청솔가지 타는 연기가 깔린다.
나라의 은혜를 입지 못한 사내들은
서로 속이고 목을 조르고 마침내는
칼을 들고 피를 흘리는데
정거장을 향해 비탈길을 굴러가는
가난이 싫어진 아낙네의 치맛자락에
연기가 붙어 흐늘댄다.
어둠이 내리기 전에 산 일번지에는
통곡이 온다. 모두 함께
죽어 버리자고 복어알을 구해 온
어버이는 술이 취해 뉘우치고
애비 없는 애기를 밴 처녀는
산벼랑을 찾아가 몸을 던진다.
그리하여 산 일번지에 밤이 오면

Hillside Lot Number One

Before the sun sets
the wind comes visiting hillside lot Number One
It shakes the roofing spread over every house,
tears the newspaper pasted on the fretwork doors,
sprinkles rock dust
over the wretched inhabitants' faces.
Once the sun has set, smoke from burning
pine branches spreads across hillside lot Number One.
Men unable to enjoy the nation's prosperity
deceive then strangle one another,
finally taking knives and shedding blood,
while smoke clings to the folds of the skirts
of women grown weary of poverty stomping their way
downhill to the railway station.
Before night falls in hillside lot Number One
there's a sound of keening. The parent
who's got hold of poisonous globefish roes
intending they should all die together
gets drunk and changes his mind after all
but the lass who's had a fatherless child
seeks out a cliff and hurls herself down.
Then as darkness comes to hillside lot Number One

대밋벌을 거쳐 온 강바람은
뒷산에 와 부딪쳐
모든 사람들의 울음이 되어 쏟아진다.

a gale that's swept over plains
strikes against the hillside behind,
turns into every person's tears and
comes pouring down.

그

눈 오는 밤에
나를 찾아 온다.
창 밖에서 문을 때린다.
무엇인가
말을 하려고 한다.

꿈속에서
다시 그를 본다.
맨발로 눈 위에 서 있는
그를.
그 발에서
피가 흐른다.

안타까운 눈으로
나를 쳐다본다.
내게 다가와서 손을
잡는다.
입속에서
내 이름을 부른다.

잠이 깨면
새벽 종이 운다.
그 종소리 속에서

He

One snowy night
he comes visiting me.
Beating at the door just outside the window.
Anxious to tell me
something.

I see him again
in my dreams.
Standing
barefoot on the snow.
Blood flows
from his feet.

He is gazing at me
with pitying eyes.
Approaching me, he grasps
my hand.
His lips
call my name.

As I awake
the dawn bell is ringing.
I can hear his voice

그의 목소리를 듣는다.
일어나
창을 열어 본다.

창 밖에 쌓인
눈을 본다.
눈 위에 얼룩진 그의
핏자국을. 그
성난 눈초리를.

within the bell's clamor.
I get up
and throw open the window.

I stare at the snow heaped
before my window.
At the stains of his blood spread
on the snow.
At his furious glare.

3月 1日

골목마다 똥오줌이 질펀이고
헌 판장이 너풀거리는 집집에
누더기가 걸려 깃발처럼 퍼덕일 때
조국은 우리를 증오했다 이 산읍에
삼월 초하루가 찾아 올 때.

실업한 젊은이들이 골목을 메우고
복덕방에서 이발소에서 소줏집에서
가난한 사람들의 음모가 펼쳐질 때
조국은 우리를 버렸다 이 산읍에
또다시 삼월 일일이 올 때.

이 흙바람 속에 꽃이 피리라고
우리는 믿지 않는다 이 흙바람을
타고 봄이 오리라고 우리는
믿지 않는다 아아 이 흙바람 속의
조국의 소식을 우리는 믿지 않는다.

계집은 모두 갈보가 되어 나가고
사내는 미쳐 대낮에 칼질을 해서
온 고을이 피로 더럽혀질 때

March 1

When every alleyway's soggy with sewage
and by each house with its shabby shaky wooden fence
tattered rags hang flapping like flags,
our country hates us. When the first day of March
visits this remote hill town.

When unemployed youths fill the alleyways
and the plots of the poor spread ever wider
in house agents' dens, barbers' shops, *soju* bars
our country rejects us. When March the first
once again comes to this remote hill town.

We do not believe that flowers will bloom
in this dust-laden wind. We do not believe
that Spring will come riding
this dust-laden wind. And alas, we do not believe
the news of our country borne on this dust-laden wind.

When the lasses have all become whores and left,
the lads gone crazy slashing at daylight
so that all the county is sullied with blood

조국은 영원히 떠났다 이 산읍에
삼월 초하루도 가고 없을 때.

our country leaves us for good.

When the first day of March

goes off and abandons this remote hill town.

서울로 가는 길

허물어진 외양간에
그의 탄식이 스며 있다
힘없는 뉘우침이

부서진 장독대에
그의 아내의 눈물이
고여 있다 가난과
저주의 넋두리가

부러진 고욤나무 썩어
문드러진 마루에
그의 아이들의
목소리가 배어 있다
절망과 분노의 맹세가

꽃바람이 불면 늙은
수유나무가 운다
우리의 피가 얼룩진
서울로 가는 길을
굽어 보며

The Road to Seoul

His sighs have soaked
into the tumble-down stable.
Helpless regrets.

On the crumbling terrace
his wife's tears
have formed pools. Ghostly voices
of poverty cursing.

The broken persimmon tree rots
and his children's voices
have permeated the rotting floor.
Oaths of despair and wrath.

When spring breezes blow, the old
suyu tree weeps.
Looking down
the road to Seoul
stained with our blood ···

이 두 개의 눈은

─ 石像의 노래

원수의 탱크에 두 팔을 먹히고
또 원수의 이빨에 혓바닥을 잘리고
이제 남은 것은 이것뿐이다 이
두 개의 눈.
누가 또다시 이것마저 바치라는가.
아무도 나에게서 이것을 빼앗지는 못한다 이
두 개의 눈은.
지켜 보리라 가난한 동포의
머리 위에 내리는 낙엽을, 흰 눈을,
그들의 종말을.
학대하는 자와 학대받는 자의
종말을 보기 위하여 내가 지닌 것은
이제 이것뿐이다 이
두 개의 눈.

This Pair of Eyes

—A statue sings

I was robbed of my two arms by an enemy tank
then my tongue was bitten off by an enemy's teeth
so now all I have left is this
pair of eyes.
Will someone tell me to give them away as well?
They'll never manage to wrest from me this
pair of eyes.
I will observe autumn leaves, snow,
their end,
falling on the heads of my poor compatriots.
All I have left now to watch the end
of oppressors and oppressed is
nothing but this
pair of eyes.

그들

쏟아지는 빗발 속을
맨발로 간다
서로 잡은 야윈 손에
멍이 맺혔다
성난 목소리로
나를 부른다
겁먹은 내 얼굴에
침을 뱉는다
흰 옷 입은 어깨에
피가 엉겼다
몰아치는 바람 속을
마구 달린다

They

They walk barefoot
through the pouring rain.
Bruises have formed
on the gaunt hands they clasped.
They call for me
in angry voices.
They spit
in my terrified face.
On their white-clad shoulders
blood has clotted.
They go rushing heedlessly
through the raging storm.

1950年의 銃殺

1

빗발이 치고 바람이 울고 총구가
일제히 불을 토한다. 통곡하라
나무여 풀이여 기억하라 살인자의
얼굴을, 대지여. 1950년 가을
죄없는 무리 2백이 차례로
쓰러질 때, 분노하라 하늘이여 이
강의 한 줄기를 피로 바꾸어라.
그러나 살인자는 끝내 도주했다.
부활하라 죄없는 무리들아, 그리하여
증언하라 이 더러운 역사를.
어둠이 깔려 시체를 묻고 비가 내려
피를 씻었다. 아무도 없는가
부활하는 자. 모두 흙속에서
원통한 귀신이 되어 우는가.

2

10년이 훨씬 지난다, 이제 그 자리엔
나라를 다스리는 높은 분네의
별장이 선다. 거실에서 부정한
거래가 이루어지고 추악한 음모가
꾀해지는 밤. 폐를 앓는 딸은
꿈을 꾼다, 맨발로 강을 건너가는

66

1950: Death by Firing-squad

1

Rain pours down, wind howls, and guns
all vomit flame. Lament now,
trees and grass! Remember the murderers' faces,
earth! That autumn of 1950
a throng of two hundred innocent souls
fell here, one by one. Rage, heavens! Transform
this river into a stream of blood.
Only finally the murderers all escaped.
Come back to life now, innocent throng, and
testify to this filthy history.
Night spread, burying the corpses; rain fell,
washing away the blood. Is there not one
that came back to life? Are they all weeping,
turned into bitter spirits under the ground?

2

Well over ten years later, on that spot now
stands the weekend bungalow of one of
our country's honored rulers. In the lounge
wicked deals are done by night, foul plots
are laid. And the weak-chested little daughter
is dreaming. Dreams of young lads wading barefoot

소년들의 꿈을. 한밤중에 눈을 뜨면
뒷수풀에서는 가마귀가 운다.
소슬한 바람이 와서 애처롭게 창을
넘본다. 아무도 없는가 부활하는 자.
그리하여 증언하는 자 아무도 없는가
이 더러운 역사를, 모두 흙속에서
영원히 원통한 귀신이 되어 우는가.

through the river. She opens her eyes in the night;
in the grove out behind, a crow is cawing.
A bleak wind comes peeping sadly through
the window. Has not one come back to life?
Then is there no one to testify?
To this filthy history? Are they all weeping,
turned for ever into bitter spirits under the ground?

3

廢鑛

그날 끌려간 삼촌은 돌아오지 않았다.
소리개차가 감석을 날라 붓던 버력더미 위에
민들레가 피어도 그냥 춥던 사월
지까다비를 신은 삼촌의 친구들은
우리 집 봉당에 모여 소주를 켰다.
나는 그들이 주먹을 떠는 까닭을 몰랐다.
밤이면 숱한 빈 움막에서 도깨비가 나온대서
칸데라 불이 흐린 뒷방에 박혀
늙은 덕대가 접어 준 딱지를 세었다.
바람은 복대기를 몰아다가 문을 때리고
낙반으로 깔려 죽은 내 친구들의 아버지
그 목소리를 흉내내며 울었다.
전쟁이 끝났는데도 마을 젊은이들은
하나하나 사라져선 돌아오지 않았다.
빈 금구덩이서는 대낮에도 귀신이 울어
부엉이 울음이 삼촌의 술주정보다도 지겨웠다.

The Abandoned Mine

Uncle was whisked off one day and never came back.
Dandelions might be blooming up on the swelling
     dumps of ore and muck deposited by trucks,
it was the usual chilly April
as uncle's friends in their sneakers
gathered in our yard and tossed back *soju.*
I could not understand why they were shaking their fists.
People said at night evil spirits emerged from
the many empty hovels; in the gloomy back room lit
dimly by a lamp I played pasteboard dump by myself.
The wind scattered slag dust before banging at the door
then howled just like my friends' father's voice —
he died crushed when the mine caved in.
The war was over but still the village lads
vanished one by one and didn't come back.
In the empty gold pit ghosts howl even in the daytime
while the sound of the owl is more revolting than
the things uncle said and did when he was drunk.

驚蟄

흙 묻은 속옷 바람으로 누워
아내는 몸을 떨며 기침을 했다.
온종일 방고래가 들먹이고
메주 뜨는 냄새가 역한 정미소 뒷방.
십촉 전등 아래 광산 젊은 패들은
밤 이슥토록 철 늦은 섰다판을 벌여
아내 대신 묵을 치고 술을 나르고
풀무를 돌려 방에 군불을 때고.
볏섬을 싣고 온 마차꾼까지 끼여
판이 어우러지면 어느새 닭이 울어
버력을 지러 나갈 아내를 위해 나는
개평을 뜯어 해장국을 시키러 갔다.
경칩이 와도 그냥 추운 촌 장터.
전쟁통에 맞아 죽은 육발이의 처는
아무한테나 헤픈 눈웃음을 치며
우거지가 많이 든 해장국을 말고.

Kyŏng-ch'ip

Lying there in just her mud-stained underwear
the wife trembled all over and kept on coughing.
All day long the underfloor flue had shaken
in that rice-mill backroom
        rank with the stench rising from soybean malt.
The young team of miners under their ten-watt lamps
started a belated game of cards lasting till late at night,
while I took the wife's place, prepared *muk*,
carried wine, fanned the fire to heat the floor.
Even the cart-boy who had come for the rice sacks
got dragged in too, the game was going fine
when suddenly the cock crowed; I collected my cut
and went to order the morning soup for the wife, who
had to go out to help carry dung. The village square
was cold though *Kyŏng-ch'ip* was past.
Old Six-toes's wife − he got shot in the war −
was there throwing wanton smiles all about her,
preparing morning soup full of cabbage leaves.

장마 뒤

그해 여름에 우리는 삼거리 금방앗간
그 앞집으로 이사를 했다. 거기다가
물감과 간수를 파는 가게를 냈다.
삼촌이 객지에서 온 광부들과 얼려
매일장취로 술만 퍼먹고 다니던
그 지겹던 가뭄을 나는 잊지 못한다.

아버지는 가게에 박혀 소주만 찾았지만
내게는 밤이 오는 것만은 즐거웠다.
길 건너 도장갈보네 집에서는
밤이 돼야만 노랫가락 소리가 들리고
나이 어린 갈보는 술꾼에게 졸리다가
우리 집으로 쫓겨와 숨어서 떨었다.

그해의 그 뜨겁던 열기를 나는 잊지
못한다. 세거리 개울가에 모여 수군대던
농군들을. 소나기가 오던 날
그들은 뿔뿔이 흩어져 도망가고
도장갈보네 집 마당은 피로 얼룩졌다.

마침내 장마가 져도 나이 어린 갈보는
좀체 신명이 나지 않는 걸까
어느날 돌연히 읍내로 떠나 버려

After the Summer Rains

In the summer that year we moved to the house
just in front of the gold mill. There
we opened a store selling dies and brine.
Uncle got on well with the miners from other parts
and I can't forget that tedious drought during which
he ended up drunk every day.

Stuck in the store, Dad could think of nothing but *soju*,
while nightfall was the only thing I enjoyed.
Across the road in the gamblers' club, once night
came you could hear sounds of singing;
when the girl had been pestered enough by drunks
she escaped to our house and hid there, trembling.

I can't forget that summer's sultry
heat. The peasants gathered muttering by the stream
at the crossroads. One rainy day
they scattered and ran in all directions,
the whorehouse yard was stained with blood.

At last, though the rains had come, that kid whore
left all of a sudden for the local town;
perhaps she wasn't having much fun any more,

집나간 삼촌까지도 영 돌아오지 않았다.
개울물이 불어 우리는 뒷산으로
피난을 가야 했고 장마가 들면
우리는 그 피비린내를 잊지 못한 채
다시 장터로 이사를 한다는 소문이었다.

she never came back, just like uncle who left home too.
The stream rose and we were forced to take refuge
on the hill behind the house; we couldn't forget
that stink of blood, and there was a rumor we'd be
moving to the market square after the rains.

그 겨울

진눈깨비가 흩뿌리는 금방앗간
그 아랫말 마찻집 사랑채에
우리는 쌀 너 말씩에 밥을 붙였다.
연상도 덕대도 명일 쇠러 가 없고
절벽 사이로 몰아치는 바람은 지겨워
종일 참나무불 쇠화로를 끼고 앉아
제천 역전 앞 하숙집에서 만난
영자라던 그 어린 갈보 얘기를 했다.
때로는 과부집으로 몰려가
외상 돼지 도로리에 한 몫 끼였다.
진눈깨비가 더욱 기승을 부리는 보름께면
객지로 돈벌이 갔던 마찻집 손자가
알거지가 되어 돌아와 그를 위해
술판이 벌어지는 것이지만
그 술판은 이내 싸움판으로 변했다.
부락 청년들과 한산 인부들은
서로 패를 갈라 주먹을 휘두르고
박치기를 하고 그릇을 내던졌다.
이 못난 짓은 오래 가지는 않아
이내 뉘우치고 울음을 터뜨리고
새 술판을 차려 육자배기로 돌렸다.
그러다 주먹들을 부르쥐고 밖으로 나오면
식모살이들을 가 처녀 하나 남지 않은

That Winter

Sleet filtered down over the gold mill and
in the guest-room of the carrier's just below it
we boarded for four bushels of rice each. Yon-sang
and Tok-taek had gone home for the holidays,
the wind driving past the cliffs was grim, all day
we sat hugging the iron stove with its oak wood fire
talking about a kid whore called Yongja we'd met
at a boarding-house in front of Chech'on station.
Sometimes we went rushing off to the widow's tavern
for a bite of pork that we chipped in to buy on credit.
At about full moon, when heavier sleet always fell,
the carrier's grandson, gone to make his fortune,
came back even poorer than before and
we held a party for him to celebrate only
the party soon turned into a fight.
The village lads and the laborers from Hansan
divided into gangs and traded blows,
knocked heads together, threw dishes about.
The unseemly conduct didn't last long;
soon they were sorry and burst into tears,
began a new party, passing glasses round
to the *Yukjabegi* beat.
When we clenched our fists and stepped outside

골짜기 광산 부락은 그대로 칠흑이었다.
쓰러지고 엎어지면서 우리들은
노래를 불러댔다. 개가 짖고 닭이
울어도 겁나지 않는 첫 새벽
진눈깨비는 이제 함박눈으로 바뀌고
산비탈길은 빙판이 져 미끄러웠다.

the valley mining village was dark as pitch; there was
not one girl left, all were off working as housemaids.
Falling down, tumbling about, we
bellowed out songs. At first light we were
not afraid though dogs barked and cocks crowed,
the sleet had now turned into a solid snowfall,
the mountain paths were treacherous, slippery with ice.

3月 1日 前後

마작판에서 주머니를 털린 새벽.
거리로 나서면 얼굴을 훑는 매운 바람.
노랭이네 집엘 들러
새벽 댓바람부터 술이 취한다.

술청엔 너저분한 진흙 묻은 신발들.
아직 해가 뜨지 않은 새벽인데도
장꾼들은 두려워 말소리를 죽이고
도살장으로 끌려 가는 돼지들이
떨면서 마구 소리를 지른다.

비틀대며 냉방으로 돌아가면
가난과 두려움으로 새파래진 얼굴을 들고
아내는 3월 1일이 오기 전에
이 못난 고장을 떠나자고 졸라 댄다.

Before and After March 1

Mahjong game, dawn, wallet empty.
Step into street, face shrivelling at biting wind.
Turn into Noraengi the miser's place.
Get drunk in a flash at daybreak.

Shabby boots thick with mud at the bar.
Still early dawn, before sunrise,
but the marketeers are silent for dread,
pigs off to the slaughterhouse
shudder and scream for all they're worth.

Go staggering into the unheated room.
Lifting a face livid with poverty and fear
the wife keeps on and on pestering: Let's leave
this dreadful place before March the First.

冬眠

누가 무슨 소리를 해도 믿을 수가 없었다
궂은 날만 빼고 아내는 매일
서울로 새로 트이는 길을 닦으러 나가고
멀건 풀죽으로 요기를 한 나는
버스 정거장 앞 만화 가게에서 해를 보냈다
친구들은 떼로 몰려와 내게 트집을 부렸다
거리로 끌어 내어 술을 퍼먹이고
갈봇집으로 앞장을 세우다가도
걸핏하면 개울가로 몰고가 발길질을 했다
곧잘 아내는 내 여윈 목을 안고 울었다
그 봄엔 유달리 흙바람이 차서
아내는 온몸이 시퍼렇게 얼어 떨었지만
나는 끝내 만화 가게에서 해를 보내며
누가 무슨 소리를 해도 믿지 않았다

Hibernation

No matter what anybody said, I could never believe them.
With the sole exception of bad days, every day the wife
went out to work on the newly cut road up to Seoul while I
staved off hunger with watery gruel and spent the year
in the cartoon shop beside the bus-stop.
From time to time my friends came flocking in to kid me.
They would drag me through the streets, force me to drink
and make me lead the way to the whorehouse
then suddenly drag me off to the stream-side and kick me.
Frequently my wife would embrace my scraggy neck and weep.
The sand-filled wind was specially cold that spring
and my wife was completely frozen, pale and shivering, but
I spent all the rest of the year in the cartoon shop
and no matter what anyone said, refused to believe them.

失明

해만 설핏하면 아랫말 장정들이
소주병을 들고 나를 찾아 왔다.
창문을 때리는 살구꽃 그림자에도
아내는 놀라서 소리를 지르고
막소주 몇 잔에도 우리는 신바람이 나
방바닥을 구르고 마당을 돌았다.
그러다 마침내 우리는 조금씩
미치기 시작했다. 소리내어 울고
킬킬대고 고래고래 소리를 지르다가는
아내를 끌어내어 곱사춤을 추켰다.
참다 못해 아내가 아랫말로 도망을 치면
금세 내 목소리는 풀이 죽었다.
윤삼월인데도 늘 날이 궂어서
아내 찾는 내 목소리는 땅에 깔리고
나는 장정들을 뿌리치고 어느
먼 도회지로 떠날 것을 꿈꾸었다.

Going Blind

Once the sun weakened, the lads from the lower village
came calling on me, bringing bottles of *soju.*
The wife used to jump and cry out if even so much
as the shade of an apricot blossom touched the window;
it took only a few glasses of *soju* to stir us up
so we stamped on the floor, pranced round the yard.
After that we would start to turn
just a little bit crazy.Weeping aloud,
giggling too and shouting out loud,
we'd drag the wife out to dance the hunchback's dance.
At last she fled to the lower village, her endurance
exhausted, at which my voice abruptly lost its power.
The weather was still bad despite the extra third month,
my voice calling the wife stayed pinned to the ground.
I dreamed I'd shaken off the lads
and was about to set off for some distant city.

歸路

온종일 웃음을 잃었다가
돌아오는 골목 어귀 대폿집 앞에서
웃어 보면 우리의 얼굴이 일그러진다
서로 다정하게 손을 쥘 때
우리의 손은 차고 거칠다
미워하는 사람들로부터 풀어져
어둠이 덮은 가난 속을 절뚝거리면
우리는 분노하고 뉘우치고 다시
맹세하지만 그러다 서로 헤어져
삽짝도 없는 방문을 밀고
아내의 이름을 부를 때
우리의 음성은 통곡이 된다

The Road Back Home

After we've lost every trace of laughter all day long
when we try to smile in front of the alley grogshop
our faces twist and contort.
When we clasp each other's hands warmly
our hands feel cold and rough.
As we limp through night-covered poverty
freed from all the people who hate us
we rage, and repent,
curse but then part,
and when we push open our rooms' curbside doors
and call our wives' names,
our voices turn into keening laments.

山邑日誌

아무렇게나 살아 갈 것인가
눈 오는 밤에 나는
잠이 오지 않는다
박군은 감방에서 송형은
병상에서 나는 팔을 벤
여윈 아내의 곁에서
우리는 서로 이렇게 헤어져
지붕 위에 서걱이는
눈소리만 들을 것인가
납북된 동향의 시인을
생각한다 그의 개가한 아내를
생각한다 아무렇게나 살아 갈
것인가 이 산읍에서
아이들의 코묻은 돈을 빼앗아
연탄을 사고 술을 마시고
숙직실에 모여 섰다를 하고
불운했던 그 시인을 생각한다
다리를 저는 그의 딸을
생각한다 먼 마을의
개 짖는 소리만 들을 것인가
눈 오는 밤에 가난한 우리의
친구들이 미치고 다시
미쳐서 죽을 때

Mountain Town Diary

Shall I go on living this slovenly life?
Sleep refuses to come
on a snowy night.
Young Park's in a cell, old Song's
in his sickbed, and I'm here beside my
skinny wife with her head pillowed on my arm,
separated from one another.
The only thing I can hear should surely be
the crunch of snow falling on the roof ?
I recall the poet from my native region
kidnapped and taken North. I recall his
remarried wife. Why should I lead such
a slapdash life? In this mountain town
I grab the kids' pocket-money
to buy coal, drink liquor,
play cards in the night-duty room.
I recall one unfortunate poet,
I recall his crippled daughter.
The only thing I can hear should surely be
dogs barking in a distant hamlet?
On snowy nights all I can hear
should surely be the sound of trains
rolling over the rails,

철로 위를 굴러 가는 기찻소리만
들을 것인가 아무렇게나
살아 갈 것인가 이 산읍에서

while our poor friends go mad,

go mad and finally die? Shall I go on living such

a slovenly life, in this mountain town?

僻地

살얼음이 언 냇물
행길 건너 술집
그날 밤에는 첫눈이 내렸다
교정에 깔리던 벽지의
좌절

숙직실에 모여
묵을 시켜 먹고
십릿길을 걸어
장터까지 가도
가난하고 어두운 밤은
아직도 멀어

서울을 얘기하고 그
더러운 허영과 부정
결식 아동 삼십 프로
연필도 공책도 없는 이
소외된 교실

잊어버리자 우리의
통곡
귀로에 깔리던
벽지의 절망
그날 밤에는 첫눈이 내렸다

The Backwoods

The lightly frozen stream,
the tavern across the road,
that night the first snow fell.
The frustration
of the backwoods lay spread across the playground.

Together in the night-duty room
ordering and eating a dish of *muk*
even after a couple of miles' walk
all the way to the market-place,
the dark poverty-stricken night
still has a long way to go.

Talking of Seoul, its
filthy pride and corruption
in this alienated classroom without
one pencil or notebook, where thirty
percent of the kids have no lunch to eat.

Let's forget our
laments,
the despair of the backwoods
buried under the homeward path.
That night the first snow fell.

4

山邑紀行

장날인데도 무싯날보다 한산하다.
가뭄으로 논에서는 더운 먼지가 일고
지붕도 돌담도 농사꾼들처럼 지쳤다.

아내의 무덤이 멀리 보이는
구판장 앞에서 버스는 섰다.
나는 아들놈과 노점 포장 아래서
외국 자본이 만든 미지근한 음료수를 마셨다.

오랜만에 보는 시골 친구들의 눈은
왜 이렇게 충혈돼 있을까.
말이 없다. 그저 손을 잡고
흔들기만 한다. 그 거짓된 웃음.

돌과 몽둥이와 곡괭이로 어지럽던
좁은 닭전 골목. 농사꾼들과
광부들의 싸움질로 시끄럽던 이발소 앞.
의용소방대원들이 달음질치던 싸전 길.

장날인데도 어디고 무싯날보다 쓸쓸하다.
아내의 무덤을 다녀 가는 내 손을
뻣뻣한 손들이 잡고 놓지를 않는다.

Mountain Town Visit

Market day, yet business is slacker than normal.
Drought, so in the fields hot dust clouds rose while
roofs, stone walls, stood weary like the laborers.

The bus stopped in front of the common market
from where the wife's grave could be seen.
Beneath a roadside stall's awning I and the boy
drank a tepid beverage produced by foreign capital.

I wonder why my hometown friends, seen again at last
after long separation, have such bloodshot eyes?
No words. Just hands clasped
and shaken. That lying smile.

The narrow chicken-shop alley
littered with stones and sticks and hoes.
In front of the barber's shop that used to ring
with farmers' and miners' quarrels.
The rice-store path where volunteer firemen used to run.

It's market day, yet everywhere is gloomier
than normal. Rough hands grasp mine as I walk
away from the wife's grave, grasp and won't let go.

시외버스 정거장

을지로 육가만 벗어나면
내 고향 시골 냄새가 난다
질퍽이는 정거장 마당을 건너
난로도 없는 썰렁한 대합실
콧수염에 얼음을 달고 떠는 노인은
알고 보니 이웃 신니면 사람
거둬들이지 못한 논바닥의
볏가리를 걱정하고
이른 추위와 눈바람을 원망한다
어디 원망할 게 그뿐이냐고
한 아주머니가 한탄을 한다
삼거리에서 주막을 하는 여인
어디 답답한 게 그뿐이냐고
어수선해지면 대합실은 더 썰렁하고
나는 어쩐지 고향 사람들이 두렵다
슬그머니 자리를 떠서
을지로 육가 행 시내버스를 탈까
육가에만 들어서면
나는 더욱 비겁해지고

Country Bus Terminal

Once past the end of Seoul's Ulchi-ro
I start to smell smells of home.
Across the muddy bus station yard
in the freezing unheated waiting room there's
an old man with ice caught in his moustache,
on closer inspection he's a neighbor from Shinni-myŏn
worrying about the piles of rice-straw
he's unable to bring in from the paddy fields,
complaining about the early cold and the icy wind.
A woman chimes in with a sigh:
Well if that's all there is to complain about ⋯
The woman keeping the tavern at the road junction:
Well if that's all there is to be anxious about ⋯
Confusion spreads, the waiting room grows colder still
and for some reason I feel afraid of the folk from home.
Shall I stealthily sneak away,
catch a bus back to Ulchi-ro?
Only once I get to Seoul's Ulchi-ro
I feel more cowardly than ever.

친구

작문 시간에 늘 칭찬을 듣던
점백이라는 애는 남양 홍씨네 산지기 자식.
협동조합 정미소에 다녀
마루 없는 토담집을 마련했단다.

봉당 멍석에까지 날아오는 밀겨.
십년만에 만나는 나를 잡고 친구는
생오이와 막소주를 내고
아내를 시켜 틀국수를 삶았다.
처녀처럼 말을 더듬는 친구의 아내.

나는 그녀의 아버지를 안다.
자전거를 타고 술배달을 하던
다부지고 신명 많던 그를 안다.
몰매 맞아 죽어 묻힌 느티나무 밑
뫼꽃 덩굴이 덮이던 그 돌더미도 안다.

그래서 너는 부끄러운가, 너의 아내가.
그녀를 닮아 숫기 없는 삼학년짜리 큰 자식이.
부엌 앞의 지게와 투박한 물동이가.

친구여. 곳집 뒤 솔나무 밭은 이제
나 혼자도 갈 수 있다.

A Friend

Spotty always used to get praised in composition class.
His father guarded the tombs of the Hongs
of Namyang. He worked at the cooperative rice-mill and
set himself up in an earth-walled house with no *maru.*

Wheat bran came wafting as far as the straw mats
in the yard. That friend, meeting me again after ten years,
grabbed me, bought cucumbers and sour *soju*
then sent his wife to boil up some *kuksu* noodles;
his wife stammered bashfully like a young girl.

I knew her father.
I knew him; he used to deliver liquor on a bicycle,
a sturdy fellow, always in high spirits.
I know that mound of stones too, covered with bindweed
under the zelkova; he was stoned to death and buried there.

Is that why you're ashamed of your wife, and your
first kid, in third grade, shy of strangers just like her?
Of the A-frame in front of the kitchen, the rough water jar?

Old friend. Nowadays I can make my way alone
to the pine grove up behind the warehouse.

나의 삼촌과 친구들이 송탄을 굽던 곳, 친구여.
밀겨와 방아 소리에 우리는 더욱 취해
어깨를 끼고 장거리로 나온다.
친구여, 그래서 부끄러운가.

That place where my cousin and his friends
used to make charcoal, old friend.
We get even more drunk surrounded by the wheat bran
　　　and the noise of the mill,
go out to the market, arms round shoulders.
Old friend, is that why you're ashamed?

時祭

1
무명 두루마기가 풍기는
역한 탁주 냄새
돗자리 위에 웅크리고 앉은 아저씨들은
꺼칠한 얼굴로 시국 얘기를 한다
그 겁먹은 야윈 얼굴들

아이들은 그래도 즐거웠다
바람막이 바위 아래 피운 모닥불에
마른 떡과 북어를 구우며
뻥뻥이를 돌고 곤두박질을 쳤다

2
—20년이 지나도 고향은
달라진 것이 없다 가난 같은
연기가 마을을 감고
그 속에서 개가 짖고
아이들이 운다 그리고 그들은
내게 외쳐 댄다
말하라 말하라 말하라
아아 나는 아무 말도 할 수가 없다

Commemorations

1

Cotton *turumagi* overcoats
stinking of *makkŏlli*
the men squatting on straw mats
were discussing the times with haggard faces.
Fearful, emaciated faces.

Still the kids were cheerful.
In a bonfire lit under a sheltering rock
they roasted stale rice-cake and dried pollack,
went racing in circles and toppling headlong.

2

— Even after twenty years the home village
hasn't altered in the least. Poverty-like
smoke holds the village wrapped
and in it dogs are barking
kids are crying and they are all
shouting at me.
Speak out! Speak out! Speak out!
Alas, there is nothing I can say.

5

갈대

언제부턴가 갈대는 속으로
조용히 울고 있었다.
그런 어느 밤이었을 것이다. 갈대는
그의 온몸이 흔들리고 있는 것을 알았다.

바람도 달빛도 아닌 것.
갈대는 저를 흔드는 것이 제 조용한 울음인 것을
까맣게 몰랐다.
—산다는 것은 속으로 이렇게
조용히 울고 있는 것이란 것을
그는 몰랐다.

A Reed

For some time past, a reed had been
quietly weeping inwardly.
Then finally, one evening, the reed
realized it was trembling all over.

It wasn't the wind or the moon.
The reed was utterly unaware that it was its own
quiet inward weeping that was making it tremble.
It was unaware
that being alive is a matter
of that kind of quiet inward weeping.

墓碑

쓸쓸히 살다가 그는 죽었다.
앞으로 시내가 흐르고 뒤에 산이 있는
조용한 언덕에 그는 묻혔다.
바람이 풀리는 어느 다스운 봄날
그 무덤 위에 흰 나무 비가 섰다.
그가 보내던 쓸쓸한 표정으로 서서
바람을 맞고 있었다.
그러나 비는 아무것도 기억할 만한
옛날이 있는 것은 아니었다. 어언듯
거멓게 빛깔이 변해 가는 제 가냘픈
얼굴이 슬펐다.
무엇인가 들릴 듯도 하고 보일 듯도 한 것에
조용히 귀를 대이고 있었다.

Graveside Epitaph

After living a lonesome life, he died.
He was buried on a quiet hill with
a stream flowing in front and a hill behind.
One warm spring day with a mild wind blowing
a white wooden marker was standing by that grave.
It stood with the same lonesome look as his life had had
exposed to every wind.
Yet that marker did not suggest a past
with nothing worth remembering. Its fragile face
that was growing darker as time went by
looked sad.
It was quietly calling attention to something
that might be heard and might be seen.

深夜

1
쓸쓸히 죽어간 사람들이여.
산정에 불던 바람이여.
달빛이여.
지금은 모두 저 종 뒤에서
종을 따라 울고 있는 것들이여.

이름도 모습도 없는 것이 되어
내 가슴속에 쌓여 오고 있는 것들이여.

2
어느날엔가
나도 그들과 같은 것이 되어
그들처럼 어디론가 쓸쓸히 돌아가리라. 그날
내가 가서 조용히 울고 있을
어느 호수여.

누군가의 슬픈 가슴이여.

Deep Night

1

All those people who ended lonesomely.
That wind that once blew on the hilltops.
That moonlight.
All those things behind the bell,
now weeping in company with the bell.

Those things deprived of name and shape,
things heaping up now in my heart.

2

One day or other
I too will turn into something like those
and like them lonesomely go back somewhere.
That lake somewhere
where on that day I shall go and quietly weep.

Someone's sad heart.

幼兒

1

창 밖에 눈이 쌓이는 것을 내어다보며 그는
귀엽고 신비롭다는 눈짓을 한다. 손을 흔든다.
어린 나무가 나무 이파리들을 흔들던 몸짓이 이러했다.

그는 모든 비밀을 알고 있는 것이다.
눈이 내리는 까닭을, 또 거기서 아름다운 속삭임들이
들리는 것을
그는 아는 것이다－충만해 있는 한 개의 정물이다.

2

얼마가 지나면 엄마라는 말을 배운다. 그것은 그가
엄마라는 말이 가지고 있는 비밀을 잃어버리는 것이다.
그러나 그는 모르고 있다.

꽃, 나무, 별,
이렇게 즐겁고 반가운 마음으로 말을 배워 가면서 그는
그들이 가지고 있는 비밀을 하나 하나 잃어버린다.

비밀을 전부 잃어버리는 날 그는 완전한 한 사람이 된다.

A Baby

1

He is gazing at the snow piling up beyond the window, his
expression says it's lovely and mysterious. He waves a hand.
Just like the baby tree used to wave its leaves.

He has knowledge of every secret.
He knows the reason why the snow falls, and the beautiful
whispering sounds it makes,
all that he knows — a replete still life.

2

In a little while he will learn the word "Mama." It means
he will lose the secret contained in the word "Mama."
But he doesn't realize that.

Flower, tree, star,
as he learns each word with a joyful, happy heart, he will
lose one by one the secrets each of them contains.

The day he loses every secret, he will become fully human.

3

그리하여 이렇게 눈이 쌓이는 날이면 그는
어느 소녀의 생각에 괴로워도 하리라.

냇가를 거닐면서
스스로를 향한 향수에 울고 있으리라.

3

Then one day with snow piling up like now he
will suffer torment at the thought of some girl.

Strolling beside the stream
he will weep, homesick for himself.

死火山 · 그 山頂에서

견딜 수 없는 안타까움이 불길이 되어 탄다.
천지가 흔들리는 폭음으로 어느날은
지각을 뚫고 솟구쳐 오른다.
미칠 듯한 희열에 아무것도 그는 모른다.
불길이 하늘 높이 솟구쳐 떨어지며
흔들리는 산.
초목은 모두 불이 되어 타고
바위는 녹아 물이 되어 흐른다.
―만 년이 지난다. 십만 년이 지난다.

보아라. 지금
불을 뿜던 분화구에는
손끝이 얼어붙도록 차고 푸른 물이 고였다.
키 작은 고산식물들이 총총히 들어선 산정엔
등산객들이 캠프를 하고 간 자리.
간간이 들리는 적적한 산새 소리가 귀에 설다.
멀리 보이는 강과 바다와 허허한 벌판.
들어 보라. 저 바람 소리.

나도 이제 불을 뿜던 분화구처럼 가슴을 헤치고

On Top of an Extinct Volcano

Unendurable frustration turns into blazing fire.
One day in an explosion shaking heavens and earth
it erupts, blasting through the earth's crust.
It is aware of nothing in that rapture of mad frenzy.
The mountain shaking
as the flames arch high into the heavens.
All the plants and trees catch fire and burn
rocks melt and flow like water.
  — Ten thousand years pass. A hundred thousand years.

Look. Now
In the crater that once spouted fire
stands a pool of water so cold it freezes the fingertips.
A host of minute mountain plants invades the top
where you can see traces of a hikers' camp.
The lonely song of a bird rings strange in the ear.
Far away glimpses of river, sea, and empty plains.
Listen. The sound of the wind.

I will force my breast open like the crater
        that once spouted fire,

온통 바람 소리로만 가슴을 채우리라.
슬픈 일이 있어도 좋다. 아아 지금 내게 무슨
괴로울 것이 있어도 좋다.

fill my breast with nothing but the sound of the wind.
Even sorrow will be fine. Even if something
should torment me it will be fine.

밤새

느티나무 밑을 도는
상여에 쫓기다가 꿈을 깬다
문득 새소리를 들었다

억울한 자여 눈을 뜨라
짓눌린 자여 입을 열라

원귀로 한치 틈도 없는
낮은 하늘을 조심스럽게 날며

저 밤새는 슬프게 운다
상여 뒤에 애처롭게 매달려
그 소년도 슬프게 운다

Night Bird

I woke from a dream where I was being
pursued by a bier round a zelkova tree.
Suddenly I heard a bird sing.

Wake up now, mistreated wretch.
Open your lips, downtrodden wretch.

Flying carefully through a lowering sky
with not a spare inch for so many resentful ghosts,

that night bird sobs so sadly.
One boy sobs sadly, too, pitifully
clinging to the back of the bier.

달빛

밤 늦도록 우리는 지난 얘기만 한다
산골 여인숙은 돌광산이 가까운데
마당에는 대낮처럼 달빛이 환해
달빛에도 부끄러워 얼굴들을 돌리고
밤 깊도록 우리는 옛날 얘기만 한다
누가 속고 누가 속였는가 따지지 않는다
산비탈엔 달빛 아래 산국화가 하얗고
비겁하게 사느라고 야윈 어깨로
밤 새도록 우리는 빈 얘기만 한다

Moonlight

We talked of old times till late at night.
The hillside inn wasn't far from the quarry.
In the yard the moonlight was bright as broad day
and we averted our eyes, ashamed even in moonlight,
as we talked far into the night about the old days.
We made no distinction between hoaxer and hoaxed.
On the slopes, daisies shone white in the moonlight
and with shoulders drooping at having lived so meanly
all night long we talked empty talk.

江

빗줄기가 흐느끼며 울고 있다
울면서 진흙 속에 꽂히고 있다
아이들이 빗줄기를 피하고 있다
울면서 강물 속을 떠돌고 있다

강물은 그 울음소리를 잊었을까
총소리와 아우성소리를 잊었을까
조그만 주먹과 맨발들을 잊었을까

바람이 흐느끼며 울고 있다
울면서 강물 위를 맴돌고 있다
아이들이 바람을 따라 헤매고 있다
울면서 빗발 속을 헤매고 있다

The River

The raindrops sob and weep.
Weeping, they pierce the muddy ground.
The children are avoiding the raindrops.
Weeping, they roam about in the river.

Could the river forget that sound of weeping?
Could it forget the sound of guns and cries?
Could it forget those tiny fists and little bare feet?

The wind sobs and weeps.
Weeping, it goes swirling over the river.
The children go wandering after the wind.
Weeping, they wander in the falling rain.

그 여름

한 사람의 울음이
온 마을에 울음을 불러 오고
한 사람의 노래가
온 고을에 노래를 몰고 왔다

구름을 몰고 오고
바람과 비를 몰고 왔다
꽃과 춤을 불러 오고
저주와 욕설과 원망을 불러 왔다

한 사람의 노래가
온 거리에 노래를 몰고 오고
한 사람의 죽음이
온 나라에 죽음을 불러 왔지만

That Summer

One person's tears
summoned tears to all the village
and one person's song
brought songs crowding into all the county.

Brought clouds crowding in,
brought wind and rain crowding in,
produced flowers and dances,
produced curses, imprecations, resentment.

One person's song
brought songs crowding into every street
and one person's death
produced death throughout the land.

누군가

누군가 나를 지켜보고 있다
새파랗게 얼어붙은 비탈진 골목길
비겁하지 않으리라 주먹을 쥐는
내 등 뒤에서 나를 비웃고 있다
그밤 나는 계집의 분냄새에도 취했었지만
1871년의 블랑키스트를 얘기하고
억울하게 죽은 내 고향 친구를 얘기했다
누군가 나를 꾸짖고 있다
잠든 아이들 옆에서 오래도록 몸을 뒤채는
아아 그리하여 저
골목을 쓰는 바람 소리에 몸을 떠는
내 등 뒤에서 나를 꾸짖고 있다
오늘밤 그 무덤 위에 눈이 내릴까
누군가 나를 지켜보고 있다

Someone

Someone is observing me.

As I clench my fists, resolved not to be afraid

in the steep alley frozen icy white

behind my back someone is mocking me. That evening

I was drunk on the smell of a girl's face-powder

but I just talked on about what Blanquist did in 1871,

talked about a hometown friend who'd died wretchedly.

Someone is rebuking me.

Yes, indeed,

rebuking me behind my back as I shudder

at the sound of the wind sweeping through that alley,

as I lie tossing beside the sleeping kids.

Is snow falling tonight upon that tomb?

Someone is observing me.

傳說

늘 술만 마시고
미쳐서 날뛰다가
마침내 그 녀석은 죽어 버렸다

내가 살던 고향 동네로
넘어가는 그 고갯길
서낭당 고목나무

빨갛고 노란 헝겊을
걸어놓고
귀신이 되어 도사리고 앉았다

안개가 낀 자욱한 여름밤
원통해서 원통해서
그 녀석은 운다

원통해서 원통해서
고목나무도 운다 그 녀석은
되살아나서 도사리고 앉았고

A Legend

He was always drinking,
he went mad, grew rowdy,
then finally the rascal died.

Up the mountain road running past
the village where I was born and bred
is an old tree that's a spirit shrine

with red and yellow strips of rag
hanging.
He became a ghost, squatting there cross-legged.

On summer nights all thick with mist
in bitterness, in bitterness
that rascal weeps.

In bitterness, in bitterness,
the old tree also weeps. That rascal
has come to life again, squatting there cross-legged.

追放

1
우리 조상들에 대한
에른스트 오페르트 그의 생각은 옳았다
강 언덕에 모여 선 헐벗은
그들에 대한 그의 생각은 옳았다
그를 미워한 것은 그들이 아니었다
페롱의 동료들을 쇠전에서 찢어 죽이고
또 그로 하여 다섯밤 다섯낮을
풀을 뜯어 먹고 살게 한
그 못된 사람들이 누구인지 우리는 안다
오페르트여 우리는 안다

2
이 어둠 속에서 친구를 원수로 생각하라
강요하는 그들은 누구인가 지금도
거짓을 참이라 우겨대는 그들은 누구인가
거리는 온통 어둠으로 덮여 있지만
오페르트여 당신을 미워하는 것은 우리가
아니다 친구를 원수로 생각하라는 저
억지 속에서 페롱의 후예들은
다시 화륜선에 실려 이 땅을 떠나고 있다
누구인가 그들을 내어몰고 있는
그자들은 누구인가

140

Exile

1

Ernst Oppert was right about our ancestors.
What he thought about them was right, as
they gathered in a ragged mob on that riverside hill.
It was not they who hated him.
We know who those wicked people were
that tore Féron's companions apart at the cattle market
then made him live for five days
and five nights on the grass he grazed.
Yes, Oppert, we know.

2

Who can they be, who demand in this dark
that we consider friends as enemies? And nowadays
who can they be who insist that lies are truth?
The streets are all covered with darkness
but Oppert, it's not we who hate you.
In the compulsion to consider friends as enemies
Féron's descendants are leaving this land again
        loaded on steamers.
Who can be the people who are driving them away,
who can they be?

우리가 부끄러워해야 할 것은

질척이는 골목의 비린내만이 아니다
너절한 욕지거리와 싸움질만이 아니다
우리가 부끄러워해야 할 것은
이 깊은 가난만이 아니다
좀체 걷히지 않는 어둠만이 아니다

팔월이 오면 우리는 들떠오지만
삐걱이는 사무실 의자에 앉아
아니면 소줏집 통걸상에서
우리와는 상관도 없는 외국의 어느
김빠진 야구 경기에 주먹을 부르쥐고
미치광이 선교사를 따라 핏대를 올리고
후진국경제학자의 허풍에 덩달아 흥분하지만
이것들만이 아니다 우리가
부끄러워해야 할 것은

이 쓸개빠진 헛웃음만이 아니다
겁에 질려 야윈 두 주먹만이 아니다
우리가 부끄러워해야 할 것은
서로 속이고 속는 난장만이 아니다
하늘까지 덮은 저 어둠만이 아니다

What We Have to be Ashamed of

It's not only the stench of muddy alleys.
It's not only petty slanging matches and fist-fights.
What we have to be ashamed of
is not only this deep poverty.
It's not only the darkness that almost never lifts.

When August comes we may be elated but
sitting on our creaky office chairs
or on a narrow bench in a *soju* bar
we clench fists about some boring baseball match
played abroad, nothing to do with us at all,
let some crazy missionary work us into a frenzy,
get excited about tall tales told by an economist
     from some underdeveloped country,
but it's not only these kinds of things
that we have to be ashamed of.

It's not only this lily-livered kind of false merriment,
it's not only our two fists shrivelled up with fear.
What we have to be ashamed of
is not only the wild way we cheat and get cheated.
It's not only the darkness that hides heaven itself.

친구여 네 손아귀에

1
창돌애비가 죽던 날은 된서리가 내렸다
오동잎이 깔린 기름틀집 바깥마당
그 한귀퉁이에 그의 시체는 거적에 싸여 뒹굴고
그의 아내는 그 옆에 실신해 누웠다

창돌이와 나는 팽이를 돌렸다
무서워서 끝내 돌아가지 못하고
싸전 마당에서 저물도록 팽이만 돌렸다

2
소주잔을 거머쥔 네 손아귀에 친구여
날카로운 칼날이 숨겨져 있음을 나는 안다
상밥집에서 또는 선술집에서 다시 만났을 때
네 눈 속에 타고 있는 불길을 나는 보았다
네 편이다 아무리 우겨대도
믿지 않는 네 어깻짓을 나는 보았다

거적에 싸인 시체 위에 떨어지던 오동잎
친구여 나는 보았다

Friend! In your Fist

1

We'd had a hard frost, the day Ch'ang-tol's Dad died.
His body lay wrapped in a mat in one corner
of the yard of the oil-press house strewn with paulownia
leaves, while his wife lay swooning beside him.

Ch'ang-tol and I played with our tops.
Too frightened to go back home we went on playing
with our tops in the rice-store yard till night fell.

2

I know that you've got a sharp knife concealed
in the fist that's clasping a *soju* glass, friend.
When we met again in the eatery and in the bar,
I saw the fire burning in your eyes.
I'm your friend. I saw your shoulders move
in disbelief, insist as I might.

Why, friend, I saw the paulownia leaves falling
on top of the straw mat wrapped round the body.

7

어둠 속에서

빗발 속에서 피비린내가 났다
바람 속에서도 곡소리가 들렸다
한여름인데도 거리는 새파랗게 얼어붙고
사람들은 문을 닫고 집 속에 숨어 떨었다

지나간 모든 죽음이 헛된 것이었을까
아이놈을 데리고 찾아간 산속
풀과 바위에는 아직도 그해의 핏자국이 보였다
한밤중에 원귀들은 일제히 깨어
통곡으로 어두운 골짜기를 뒤덮었으나

친구여 나는 무엇이 이렇게 두려운가
답답해서 아이놈을 깨워 오줌을 누이고
기껏 페르 라셰즈 묘지의 마지막 총소리를
생각했다 허망한 그 최초의 정적을

보라 보라고 내 눈은 외쳐대고
들으라 들으라고 내 귀는 악을 썼지만
이 골짜기에 얽힌 사연을
안다는 것이 나는 부끄러웠다

험한 바위 설기에 친구를 묻고
흙 묻은 손을 비벼 털고서

In the Dark

A stench of blood arose in the falling rain.
And sobbing could be heard in the wind.
It was summer yet the streets were frozen white,
folks shut their gates, shuddered hidden indoors.

Could all those past deaths have been in vain?
That year's bloodstains shone on grass and rocks
up in the hills where I had taken the kids.
Deep at night all the grieving spirits would wake
and fill the dark valley with their keening laments.

Tell me, friend, what am I so afraid of?
I was so anxious that I woke the kid to go for a piss,
and recalled vividly the last shot in Père Lachaise
Cemetery. My eye shouted: Look, look!

My ear screamed: Listen, listen,
to the very first empty stillness
but I felt ashamed to admit that I knew
the tales entangled in that mountain valley.

We buried our friend in the lee of a rock
then scrubbed and wiped our muddy hands

우리는 비로소 우리의 힘을 알았다 한
그 지나간 모든 죽음이 헛된 것이었을까

꽃잎에서도 이슬방울에서도
피의 통곡이 들리는 한여름밤
친구여 무엇이 나는 이렇게 두려운가

wondering if really all those past deaths had been in vain,
that had taught us just how strong we were?

In this summer night loud with the keening of blood
in flowers, yes, and in dewdrops, too,
tell me friend, what am I so afraid of?

山驛

여관방 미닫이를 석탄가루가 날아와 때렸다
철길 위를 삐꺽거리는 탄차 소리에 눈을 뜨면
거기 사슬에 묶인 친구들의 손이 어른대고
좁은 산역은 날이 새어 술렁대었다

이 외진 계곡에 영 봄이 오지 않으리라는
뜬소문만 전봇줄에 엉겨붙어 윙윙대는
작은 변전소 옆 허술한 어전 골목

본바닥 젊은이들은 눈이 뒤집혀 나그네를 뒤졌지만
죽음보다 더 두려운 것이
무엇인가를 생각하는 내 귀에

번개가 머리칼을 태우고 천둥이 귀를 찢어도
겁내지 말라 외쳐대는 친구들의
고함소리가 들리고 노랫소리가 들렸다
이제 저 싸늘한 새벽별이 우리 편이 아니더라도

Mountain Station

Flying coal dust rattled at the inn room's door.
Eyes opening to the screech of coal-trains
retained an image of the hands of friends chained there
while the small station was astir from daybreak.

A shabby fish-shop alley by a humming substation
that sent into the power lines only false reports
that spring would never come to this isolated valley.

Local youths went crazy and searched travellers
while I wondered what on earth might be
more frightening than death and in my ear

friends' shouts could be heard, songs could be heard,
yelling not to be afraid, though
lightning scorched my hair, thunder split my ears.
Even if that icy morning star was no longer on our side.

대목장

살아 있는 것이 부끄러워
내 모습은 초췌해 간다

뜯기운 수려선 연변
작은 면 소재지
추운 대목장

저 맵찬 바람 소리에도
독기어린 수근댐에도
나는 귀를 막았다

아는 사람을 찾아
왼종일 장거리를 돈다

Year's-End Fair

I'm looking increasingly haggard,
ashamed of being alive.

Along the now dismantled rails
a little county town
a cold year's-end fair.

I shut my ears
to the sound of the biting wind
to whispers full of malice.

All day long I wandered through the market alleys
hoping to find someone I knew.

邂逅

그 여자는 내 얼굴을 잊은 것 같다
정거장 앞 후미진 골목 해장국집
우리는 서로 낯선 두 나그네가 되어
추탕과 막걸리로 요기를 했다

그 공사장까지는 백리라 한다
가을비에서는 여전히 마른 풀내가 나고
툇마루에 모여 음담으로 날궂이를 하던
버들집 소식은 그 여자도 모른다 한다

변전소에 직공으로 다니던
그 여자의 남편은 내 시골 선배였다
벅구를 치며 잘도 씨름판을 돌았지만
이상한 소문이 떠돌다가 과부가 된
그 여자는 이제 그 일도 잊은 것 같다

메밀꽃이 피어 눈부시던 들길
숨죽인 욕지거리로 술렁대던 강변
절망과 분노에 함께 울던 산바람

우리가 달려온 길도 그 노랫소리도
그 여자는 이제 다 잊은 것 같다
끝내 낯선 두 나그네가 되자고 한다

A Chance Encounter

That woman seems to have forgotten my face.
In a *haejang* soup place down a lonely alley
by the bus stop, strangers to one another now,
we satisfied our hunger with loach soup and *makkŏlli*.

They say it's thirty miles to that construction site.
That woman really knows no news of the wine house
where we sat on the bench cracking filthy jokes
while autumn showers stirred up a smell of dry grass.

Her husband was a mechanic in the substation;
he was older than me, from the same village.
He banged the *pokku* at wrestling matches
but then strange rumors spread and she became a widow
though the woman seems to have forgotten that too.

The field paths bright with buckwheat flowers,
the riverside alive with whispered oaths,
mountain winds moaning too in despair and rage,

the path we hurried along, that sound of singing:
the woman seems to have forgotten all that too, now.
Let's just be two strangers, two separate travellers,

내려치는 비바람 그 진흙길을
나 혼자서만 달려 나가라 한다

she seems to insist.
I'll have to hurry all alone back down that muddy road
in the driving rain.

同行

그 여자는 열살 난 딸 얘기를 했다
그 신고 싶어하는 흰 운동화와
도시락 대신 싸 가는 고구마 얘기를 했다

아침부터 가랑비가 왔다
명아주 깔린 주막집 마당은 돌가루가 하얗고
나는 화장품을 파는 그 여자를 향해
실실 헤픈 웃음을 웃었다

몸에 밴 그 여자의 비린내를 나는 몰랐다
어물전 그 가난 속에 얽힌 얘기를 나는 몰랐다

느린 벽시계가 세 시를 치면
자다 일어난 밤대거리들이 지분댔다
활석 광산 아래 마을에는
아침부터 비가 오고

우리는 어느새 동행이 되어 있었다
우리가 가고 있는 곳이 어딘지를
그러나 우리는 서로 묻지 않았다

Travelling Companions

That woman talked about her nine-year-old daughter.
She talked about the white running shoes she wanted
and the sweet potatoes she carried in place of lunch.

It had been drizzling since early morning.
The tavern yard full of weeds was white with dust
and I smiled silly wanton smiles
at that woman who was selling beauty-products.

I knew nothing then of the way her body stank.
nothing of the talk being spun in the poverty
        of the dried fish store.

When the clock on the wall, slow, struck three
the night crew, already awake, kept pestering her.
In the village beneath the steatite mine
it had been raining since early morning.

We suddenly became travelling companions.
We had no idea where each was going
yet neither of us asked the other.

處署記

여름 들어 나는 찾아갈 친구도 없게 되었다
사글세로 든 시장 뒤 반찬가게 문간방은
아침부터 찌는 것처럼 무덥고 종일
아내가 뜨개질을 하러 나가 비운 방을 지키며
나는 내가 미치지 않는 것이 희한했다
때로 다 큰 쥔집 딸을 잡고
객쩍은 농지거리로 핀퉁이를 맞다가
허기가 오면 미장원 앞에 참외를 놓고 파는
동향 사람을 찾아가 우두커니 앉았기도 했다
우리는 곧잘 고향의 벼 농사 걱정을 하고
떨어지기만 하는 소값 걱정을 하다가도
처서가 오기 전에 어디 공사장을 찾아
이 지겨운 서울을 뜨자고 별러댔다
허나 봉지쌀을 안고 들어오는 아내의
초췌하고 고달픈 얼굴은 내 기운을 꺾었다
고향 근처에 수리조합이 생긴다는 소문이었지만
아내의 등에 업혀 잠이 든 어린 것은
백일이 지났는데도 좀체 웃지 않았다
처서는 또 그냥 지나가 버려 동향사람은
군고구마 장사를 벌일 채비로 분주했다

Diary Entry for *Ch'ŏsŏ* Day

By early summer I had no friends left to visit.
The grocer's room we rented behind the market was so
hot it seemed to steam by early morning and
all day long I guarded the room the wife left empty,
going out to knit, marvelled that I had not gone mad.
Sometimes I would crack a joke with the owner's big daughter
and get scolded for my pains.
If I was hungry I would visit the locals selling *ch'amoi* melons
in front of the beauty parlor and idly squat there.
First we would worry about the rice harvest back home,
then worry about the price of livestock all the time falling,
then decide to find a construction job before Ch'ŏsŏ came
so as to get away from this wretched Seoul.
But then the wife's haggard, weary face as she came in
clutching a bag of rice squashed all such thoughts.
A rumor said an irrigation association was to be set up
near my home village but the baby asleep on the wife's back
hardly ever smiled though it was over a hundred days old.
Ch'ŏsŏ went by unnoticed in late August and soon people
were preparing to sell baked sweet potatoes in winter streets.

골목

이발 최씨는 그래도 서울이 좋단다
자루에 기계 하나만 넣고 나가면
봉지 쌀에 꽁치 한 마리를 들고 오는
그 질척거리는 저녁 골목이 좋단다
통걸상에 앉아 이십원짜리 이발을 하면
나는 시골 변전소 옆 이발소에 온 것 같다
술독이 오른 딸기코와 떨리던 손
늦 어린애를 배어 뒤뚱거리던 그의 아내
최씨는 골목 안 생선 비린내가 좋단다
쉴 새 없는 싸움질과 아귀다툼이 좋단다
이발소에 묻혀 묵은 신문이나 뒤적이고
빗질을 하고 유행가를 익히고
허구한날 우리는 너무 심심하고 답답했지만
최씨는 이 가파른 산동네가 좋단다
시골보다도 흐린 전등과 앰프소리가 좋단다
여자들이 얼려 잔돈 뜯을 궁리나 하고 돌아가는
동네에 깔린 가난과 안달이 좋단다
그 딸기코의 병신 아들의 이름은 무엇이던가
사경을 받으러 다니던 딸의 이름은 무엇이던가
어느 남쪽 산골 읍내에서 여관을 했다는
이발 최씨는 그래도 서울이 좋단다
골목에서 모여드는 쪼무래기 손님들과
극성스럽고 억척같은 어머니들이 좋단다

164

An Alley

Ch'oi the barber reckons Seoul's fine all the same.
The muddy evening alley's fine,
where he comes home carrying rice and a mackerel
if only he goes out with his clippers in a bag.
Sitting on his stool having a twenty-Won haircut is
like being in the barber's by the village substation.
His nose all red, his hands trembling from drink,
his wife tottering about in a belated pregnancy,
Ch'oi reckons the alley with its stench of fish is fine.
The ceaseless squabbles and bickering are fine.
Hid in the barber's browsing old papers,
combing our hair and practicing songs,
the days go by and we might be bored, frustrated,
yet Ch'oi reckons our steep hillside slum's fine.
The light and radio's dimmer than home : it's fine.
The poverty and pain of the slum are fine,
where women wander about in search of some cash.
What was the name of that drunkard's crippled son?
What's his daughter's name, always collecting bills?
Ch'oi once ran an inn far to the south
yet still he reckons Seoul is fine.
The kids swarming in the alley whose hair he cuts
and their tough impatient mothers are all just fine.

우리는 다시 만나고 있다

삐걱이는 강의실 뒷자리에서
이슬 깔린 차가운 돌 층계 위에서
우리들은 처음 만났다
경상도 전라도
그리고 충청도에서 온 친구들
비와 바람과 먼지 속에서
처음 우리는 손을 잡았다
아우성과 욕설과 주먹질 속에서

충무로 사가 그 목조 이층 하숙방
을지로 후미진 골목의 대폿집
폐허의 명동
어두운 지하실 다방
강의실에 찌렁대던
노교수의 서양사 강의
토요일 오후 도서관의 정적
책장을 넘기면 은은한
전차 소리

그해 겨울 나는 문경을 지났다
약방에 들러 전화를 건다
달려 나온 친구
분필가루 허연 커다란 손

We Meet Again

We first met
in the squeaky back seat of the classroom
up the cold dew-sodden stone stairs.
Mates from Kyŏngsang and Chŏlla
as well as Ch'ungch'ŏng provinces,
we first grasped hands in friendship
in rain and wind and dust.
In shouts and curses and fisticuffs.

Our second-floor wooden rented room in Ch'ungmu-ro,
the grog-house down that obscure alley in Ulchi-ro,
the ruins of Myŏng-dong,
dark basement cafés ,
that old professor's lectures on western history
echoing in the classroom,
the silence in the library on Saturday afternoons
the distant roar of trams
as you turned a page.

In winter that year I was passing through Munkyŏng
so I turned into the chemist's and made a phone call.
A friend came dashing out,
his great hands white with chalk,

P는 강원도 어느 산읍에서
생선가게를 한단다 K는
충청도 산골에서 정미소를 하고
이제 우리는 모두 헤어져
공장에서 광산에서 또는 먼 나라에서

한밤중에 일어나 손을 펴 본다
우리의 핏속을 흐르는 것을
본다 솟구쳐 오는 아우성 소리
어둠 속에 엉겨드는 그것들을 본다
제주도 강원도 경기도에서
비와 바람과 먼지 속에서
향수와 아쉬움과 보람 속에서

he said one was up in some Kangwŏn mountain town
running a fish shop, while another was in charge
of a rice mill in a remote Ch'ungch'ŏng village.
We're all scattered far and wide now,
in factories, mines, even in distant countries,

we get up in the night and hold out a hand,
we look to see what's flowing in our blood,
we see things clotting in the dark:
the noise of shouting blazing up
in Cheju and Kangwŏn and Kyŏnggi provinces
in rain and wind and dust,
in nostalgia, dissatisfaction, and fruitfulness.

『한국문학 영역총서』를 펴내며

한국문학을 본격적으로 번역하여 해외에 소개하는 일이 필요함을 우리는 오래 전부터 절실히 느껴 왔다. 그러나 좋은 번역을 만나기는 좋은 창작품을 만나는 것 못지 않게 어렵다. 운이 좋아서 좋은 번역이 있을 경우에는 또한 출판의 기회를 얻기가 쉽지 않다. 서구의 유수한 출판사들은 시장성을 앞세워 지명도가 높지 않은 한국의 문학작품을 출판하기를 꺼린다. 한국문학의 지명도가 높아지려면 먼저 훌륭하게 번역된 작품들이 세계적인 명성이 있는 출판사에서 출판이 되어 널리 보급이 되어야 하는데, 설혹 훌륭한 번역이 있다 하더라도 이 작품들이 해외에서 출판될 기회가 극히 제한되어 있어서, 지명도를 높일 길이 막막해지는 악순환을 거듭하는 것이 현실이다. 이런 현실을 타개하는 길은 좋은 작품을 제대로 번역하여 우리 손으로 책답게 출판하여 세계의 독자들에게 내놓는 데서 찾을 수밖에 없다. 이런 일을 하기 위해 도서출판 답게에서 "한국문학 영역총서"를 세상에 내놓는다.

「답게」영역총서는 한영 대역판으로 출판되며, 이 총서는 광범위한 독자층을 위하여 만들어진 것이다. 무엇보다도 이 총서를 통해 해외의 많은 문학 독자들이 한국문학을 알게 되기를 희망한다. 이 총서는 또한 국내외에서 한국학을 공부하거나 영어로 번역된 한국 작품을 필요로 하는 영어 사용권의 모든 사람들과 한국문학의 전문적인 번역자들을 위한 것이기도 하다. 전문 번역인들은 동료 번역자들의 작업을 자신들의 것과 비교함으로써 보다 나은 새로운 번역 방법을 모색할 수 있을 것이다. 고급한 영어를 배우기를 원하는 한국의 독자들도 대역판으로 출간되는 이 총서를 읽음으로써, 언어가 어떻게 문학적으로 신비롭게 또 절묘하게 쓰이는지를 깨닫는 등 많은 것을 얻을 수 있을 것이다.

아무리 말쑥하게 잘 만들어진 책이라도 그 내용이 신통치 않으면 결코 책다운 책일 수 없다는 자명한 이유에서, 「답게」 영역총서는 좋은 작품을 골라 최선의 질로 번역한 책만을 출판할 것이다. 또한 새로운 번역자의 발굴과 격려가 이 총서 발간의 목적 가운데 하나이다. 답게 출판사가 발행하는 이 총서가 한국문학의 번역의 중요성을 다시 한 번 일깨우고, 문학작품의 번역이라는 불가능한 꿈을 가능하게 하려는 번역자들의 노력에 보탬이 되기를 바란다. 이런 시도가 여러 가지로 유용하고 또 도전적인 것이 될 때, 더 나아가서는 잘 번역된 한국 작품의 전세계적인 출판 작업이 이루어지는 단초를 마련할 수 있을 때, 이 선구적인 계획은 진정으로 성공적인 것이 될 것이다.

김 영 무 (서울대 영문과 교수)

Series Editor's Afterword

Extensive translation of Korean literature for the foreign readers has for many years been felt a pressing need. But to fall upon a good translation is much harder than to discern a good original work. If we are fortunate enough to secure a good translation, it is often very difficult to get it published abroad.

The major publishers of the western world are not yet prepared to run the risk of publishing works of relatively unknown Korean literature. Yet if Korean literature is to achieve worldwide fame, it first of all needs to be well translated, and then put into circulation throughout the world by those very publishers which are so reluctant to publish even good translations of Korean literature. It is a vicious circle : no publication without fame but no fame without publication. To save the situation, we should perhaps try to make available to readers abroad choice translations we ourselves have published in editions of high quality. The DapGae English Translations of Korean Literature series has been launched with this aim.

Each volume of the DapGae series will be a bilingual edition. We expect a wide-ranging audience for the series. It is our primary hope that it will help introduce many foreign readers to the world of Korean literature. The series is especially intended to serve English-speaking students enrolled in Korean studies programs and all who need translations of Korean literature, as well as those who may wish to compare their own translations with the translations of fellow translators in order to find new and better ways of translating. Korean readers studying advanced English can also benefit from reading these bilingual editions : the experience may help them to recognize the mystery of true mastery of the literary use of language.

However well designed a book may be, it cannot properly serve its purpose if the contents are mediocre. For that reason, the DapGae series will strive to introduce to the readers of the world the best translations of the finest works of Korean literature. One of the objectives of the series is to find and encourage new talents in English translation. We hope that the DapGae English Translations of Korean Literature series will serve in some small way to refocus attention upon the importance of translating Korean literature into good English and to make possible the impossible dream of literary translation. This pioneering project will be a true success not only if it proves useful and challenging but also if it paves the way for the publication of fine translations of Korean literature on a worldwide scale.

Young-Moo Kim
Department of English
Seoul National University

저자와의
협의 하에
인지 생략

농 무

펴낸이 / 一庚 張少任
옮긴이 / 안선재, 김영무
지은이 / 신경림

펴낸곳 / 도서출판 답게

초판인쇄일 / 1999년 2월 25일
초판발행일 / 1999년 3월 2일
주소 / 137-064 서울시 서초구 방배 4동 829-22호
원빌딩 201호
등록 / 1990년 2월 28일, 제 21-140호
전화 / 편집 591-8267, 532-4867
영업 596-0464, 537-0464
팩시밀리 / 594-0464
ISBN 89-7574-101-X 02810
원작판권 : ⓒ 신경림
번역판권 : ⓒ 안선재 , 김영무

나답게 · 우리답게 · 책답게
값 7,000원
잘못된 책은 바꾸어 드립니다.

이 책은 Cornell East Asia Series No. 105로, 도서출판 답게와
Cornell East Asia Series와의 공동출판 형식으로 나온 것임을 밝힙니다.